SIMPLY
SPIRITUAL

Small to medium!
The life of a psychic.

JACQUELINE ROGERS

ISBN 978-1-907203-69-5

Typesetting by Wordzworth Ltd
www.wordzworth.com

Cover design by Titanium Design Ltd
www.titaniumdesign.co.uk

Printed by Lightning Source UK
www.lightningsource.com

Cover image by Nigel Peace

Published by Local Legend
www.local-legend.co.uk

For my brothers, who shared the most difficult part of my journey with me.

Graham, in the spirit world since 1997.

Martin, in the spirit world since 2008.

Andy, in America and so far away.

I miss you all.

This book

This book is about the human journey, about finding our true paths in life.

All too often we feel very small, as if our lives are insignificant compared to the vastness of the universe. We are here and then we are gone. Do we mean anything at all, and is there any purpose? These are the greatest questions that we face, especially when we suffer the grief of losing a loved one.

But in this, Jacqueline Rogers' uplifting and often astonishing debut book, we learn that being human is a very special thing and that our spirits are far from being small. She describes her very personal experiences with great courage. As a healer, she shows us the power of spiritual energy. And in her work as a medium, she brings not only genuine comfort to the bereaved but equally inspiration to us all, to see the meaningfulness of life's challenges and to become the best that we can be.

Above all, Jacqueline's story proves to us that we are loved and that we do not walk our paths alone.

Jacqueline Rogers was brought up in Leamington Spa. She now lives in Warwickshire with her husband, her two sons and their cat. The spirit world has been contacting her since she was eight years old, and not by her choice!

Her website is *www.simplyspiritual.org.uk*

Acknowledgements

I offer my gratitude and love to so many people. To my dearest friends Tob, Sandie and Chrissie, to Lilian for pushing me so hard, to Mark my teacher and brother, and to Martha who literally made me write it down and supported me every step of the way. To Ray without whose love, support and hard work I would not have found the courage to continue. To Daniela, my technical guru. To my Mum, who told me to write it just as it was, and to my husband for supporting and loving me just as I am. To Eileen, with thanks for being you, a promise completed.

I thank all the spiritual places I have worked in, the thousands of people who have come to see me work over the years, and all my beautiful friends in the spirit world who guide me daily and never give up on me. I give thanks for my sons Elliott and Thomas, who are my greatest success.

Mostly I thank my Daddy, that I could be part of his journey and he part of mine, making my life perfect for six years. I thank him for his patience in the past forty-three years, when he has been with me but I was too blind to see.

May spirit bless you all and keep you safe in the arms of those you love.

Contents

Foreword

A friend of mine once said to me that the work I do as a medium can mean the difference between hope and sorrow. She described grief as being like a long, dark and damp corridor that is lonely, scary and seemingly never ending. But then she said that a conversation with me changed everything, and it was as if an 'Exit Ahead' sign suddenly lit up in the corridor. She told me that being a medium is a great gift and that ten minutes of my time can bring solace to someone's soul – so I should try to reach out to as many people as I possibly can.

I wrote this book as I was asked to do by the spirit world, for all of you - to give you hope in the darkest of situations, to help you to find the strength to overcome pain and anguish and replace it with love and understanding, to somehow make sense of the experiences that you have on this side of life and to know that others have been there before you. You may never understand totally, but with time comes acceptance of the beautiful person that is you.

"Small is beautiful" says Schumacher. The key is to remember that no matter how much more you become in the world of people around you, you are always just part of the infinite plan. Maintain that thought and you could be bigger than you ever thought possible. Don't buy into scenarios that promise to make you 'more important', as that will eclipse the true you, the beautiful you.

Know that you are never alone in this world and you are always loved by forces unseen. There are forces that love and guard you, no matter who or what you are. That is very important to understand, no matter what happens to you and what path you find yourself on – there are no exceptions. So trust your heart, love yourselves first and treat it as gently as you would a child. Honour yourselves first, and then give to others; miracles can happen and you will find your 'more'.

The role of a medium is exactly how it sounds – the middle man or woman. I am not special in any way. I am human. I am me. I love to laugh - humour is in all places, even the darkest ones where you believe no light exists. As we travel through our lives we soon learn that this is one of the strongest gifts we possess. It has the ability to push all other feelings aside in its bid to fill our lives, so let it do so. I use that energy to connect like a telephone from this world to the next, in order to prove there is life after death.

A very long time ago I was asked by a lovely man in the spirit world who I was. I said, after some thought, "A mother, and a wife" and I was told, "No, that is what you do, not who you are." I couldn't answer any further. I didn't really understand the question, to be honest. Now I do, although it took years of searching and utter confusion. It's a search that you can only complete yourself. It has taken me many years to become a good medium. The journey is tough but beautiful, and everything I have experienced has made me who I am. I am imperfect, as we all are, but I'm content with that.

In this book I describe my journey to the point that I am at now. I talk a little about spiritual philosophy and offer an insight to the world of spirit, as both worlds are connected, one around the other. There are plenty of books that describe what happens when you get to the other side; that is not what this book is about. It is about the human journey, about finding your way, your truth; but also about knowing that we are not alone travelling along this path and how to understand that, and to find the possibilities that exist for each of us and within each of us. Someday, hopefully, we shall all be able to see, sense and experience its beauty in our lives.

I hope that my story helps you to understand, in your own way, and to believe a little of something more.

Prologue

My eyes flickered open but it wasn't morning. Why was I awake? I heard a noise and saw a shadow in my room. "Oh, no! No, it's not happening again. Please, no." I prayed that I was still asleep and that I could close my eyes and when I woke up it would be morning. I told myself that I was imagining it, it was just a dream, the vivid imagination of an eight year old – that's what my mother said whenever I tried to tell her about it.

There it was again. A bolt of fear stabbed through me. My heart rate sped up. My hearing sharpened, the fuzzy security of sleep had vanished. It was 2.40 a.m. and my bed was shaking. My eyes shot open and I didn't move an inch, not daring to breathe. My heartbeat was drumming in my ears and I felt pure terror. Someone was walking around my bedroom. It was a man. I didn't know him. Then I heard the noise again, the most awful noise. Someone was climbing the stairs, slowly, rhythmically, with deep rasping breathing sounds in time with each heavy step taken.

Oh, no! It's going to get me! I put my fingers in my ears but I could still hear it. I started whimpering. I sat up on the side of my bed, hugging myself as I shook with absolute terror and the certainty that it would get me this time. Grandmother, with whom I shared my room, stirred and blinked open her eyes as if she had been woken by something – could she have heard it too? My frightened, glaring eyes stared at her and her face said it all. I could see initial shock, disbelief, then a knowing look on her face - did she understand what it was? She saw my feeble form shaking and the petrified look on my face and threw back the covers of her bed and hurried over to me; grabbing me in a protective hug she said, "Don't worry, they won't hurt you."

I had so many questions that I wanted to ask. "What is it? Who won't hurt me? Why do I keep hearing it?" But all I could do was collapse sobbing with relief into her nightdress and she rocked me and stroked my head with soothing words of comfort. At last I wasn't alone.

When I eventually calmed down and my heaving sobs and hiccups had abated, my grandmother sat on her bed facing me. She took my hands in hers and told me not to be afraid. She said that the noises wouldn't hurt me. I asked her to tell me what they were and how she knew they wouldn't hurt me. She was careful not to say any words that would scare me, but I knew what she meant. She said that they wanted to be with me, to protect me. I was confused and thought 'But who are they? And why do I need protecting? And if they are there to protect me, why do they scare me so much?' I asked her who it was, hoping she would know. She just calmly said, "I don't know".

Her explanation didn't help me at all really, because I just wished these 'ghosts' would go off and haunt someone else and leave me alone. I knew that there was more to it than just a noisy spirit - there was something deeper going on. I still didn't understand why it was happening to me though, and my grandmother could not, or would not, answer that question. I didn't mind that so much though, because I was just so relieved there was someone else who knew what I was talking about. Someone else who understood the fear and confusion I was feeling. I felt so relieved by the knowledge that it wasn't just my imagination and someone knew that I wasn't mad and that I wasn't making it up. In those moments of abject fear I wanted it all to stop so badly, but little did I know that all those terrifying experiences would shape my future so significantly.

CHAPTER ONE

The Very Beginning

I want to tell you how and why it all began, and I want you to see the similarities within your own lives, to know that the experiences we have right from the beginning mould us into the people we need to be. I am grateful for them now, but it was not always like this. So let's start…

My journey began in 1963 when I was born in the middle of England, the fourth child of Pat and Cyril, and younger sister to three brothers, Graham, Martin and Andy. We were an ordinary family, in an ordinary town. My Mum was a housewife and Dad worked for an electronics company in the local city.

I don't remember much about those early days, but I'm told I was a very mischievous child pretty much as soon as I could walk. I was small for my age, did not eat well, was really inquisitive and would not do as I was told - I had such a convincing angelic face then! It seems that I have always been the same, going my own way, carrying on regardless.

There were the usual sibling squabbles and whatever we did wrong Andy always took the blame. He was Mummy's boy and we always coerced him into being the fall guy as he could get away with any misdemeanour. We didn't know why, we just thought she liked him more. I found out why many years later - when he was a small boy Andy had accidently knocked a bowl off a table and it smashed onto the floor, cutting the whole of his finger open. It was never straight after that. Mum never forgave herself.

Spending time with my brothers was the best! My brothers were great fun. Graham was the eldest, had a mop of blond hair and he was the quiet one, five years older than me. Then there was Martin, who was the loud, noisy one – always the centre of attention and larger than life, two years older. I was closest to Andy - there is only eighteen months between us. I was always comfortable in their company, even though they would torment me terribly. Being the only girl made me tough, though. As time went on, having a protective older brother was very useful, especially when people bullied me at school. I was not knowingly aware at this point of my life that I would be any different. There was nothing exceptional about me.

I was definitely a Daddy's girl, all the way. He'd always wanted a girl and after three boys there was great excitement when I arrived. My Nan always told me that he wanted a girl so much, he already had the name of Jacqueline Ann picked out. Now it's only used when I am in trouble; mind you, come to think of it, I always have been.

Dad was my whole world and I adored him completely. Of course I loved my Mum but I really wanted to be with Dad every minute of every day. Every work day, around tea time, I would sit with my nose pressed up against the window of the front door. It was opaque glass and I waited and watched for the familiar blob through the window which grew as he pulled up closer to the house. I knew his car so well. I loved that big smile, his hugs. We had such a strong bond. Mum was so busy - can you imagine having the responsibility of four children under the age of five to raise? She deserved a medal.

Dad was a musician and he played the double bass in dance bands all through the forties and fifties. The bass had its own special place in the corner of the hallway wrapped in a rough cloth cover. Occasionally he would play for my brothers and me. He used to thrum the bass like drums and we would run around him, whooping and howling, pretending to be

Indians, building a wigwam in the lounge out of cushions from the sofa. Sundays were special for me and my Dad, it was our day. He would cook the lunch and then take us all out somewhere, usually to the park, to give Mum some respite. I always liked to sit on the coin-operated pink elephant in the park, but once was never enough; simple pleasures; simple memories. Returning home, it was bath time. After that came my favourite hours, when I would sit curled up in the chair with him. Even now I can remember that feeling, and nothing touches it to this day. I lay in his arms. Sunday was a time when I could have warm hugs with my Daddy, looking up at him, with his big blue eyes and his slightly addled smile.

Nothing else mattered in my small life, he was everything to me. My life then was idyllic and wonderful. I was happy, well cared for and everything was warm and safe, right up until I was six years old. We would have idyllic summers playing in the sunshine and winters playing in the snow.

Dad developed a cough which was too persistent, so Mum eventually persuaded him to contact the doctor who decided further tests were required at hospital. Shortly after this all our lives changed forever. Mum received a `phone call from the doctor, telling her that Dad was very ill and needed to go to hospital immediately. She rang him at work; he came straight home and when he arrived they just held each other. She told him he would be ok, he would beat it; he never replied.

I was too young to really understand what was wrong, but I knew that Dad always had a cigarette in his hand. He always smelled of smoke, always had. It was part of him and he always walked around with a cigarette hanging out of his mouth for as long I could remember. He'd been diagnosed with lung cancer. He was very ill but he wanted to carry on as normal and kept going to work until he was told he must leave work to receive treatment. When he was in hospital, I used to sit for hours on the bed next to him, keeping him company and holding the basin and his toothbrush while he washed his face and hands. It was such an important job to me, to help; I wanted to be there with him and it was just natural.

The doctor had prescribed some experimental drugs that gradually took away the use of his legs. In effect he was paralysed from the waist down. Eventually it became obvious that he would have to stay in bed permanently, so a bed was brought into the lounge. It was one of those old metal hospital beds that used to have a pulley and a chain to raise you up. It rattled. I used to hear that noise in bed and it was a comforting kind of sound; that's where he stayed until the end. We all adapted to Dad being downstairs very quickly; he was in his bed in the lounge and we would sit around him, watching TV together or chatting about what we did at school. He was there, and that's how it was, it was normal.

The fact that Dad would die was never discussed with me, not by him nor anyone else. Nobody sat down with my brothers and me and explained what it meant, or what would happen, or why it was happening. Then about a month before he died I was upstairs sleeping and I had a very vivid dream.

A Chinese gentleman came to me and told me that my Dad was going to die, as it was his time to leave. I understood exactly what he meant, there was no ambiguity. I was standing in a beautiful garden and he walked up to me, bent down and said it. I remember us staring deeply and meaningfully into each other's eyes; he was full of knowledge, full of love. He spoke to me like it was a very normal conversation. I didn't know this man, but he sure knew me.

I woke up with a start and burst into huge sobbing tears. I scrambled out of bed, went running downstairs and threw the door open into the lounge. I leapt onto Dad's bed and lay in his arms sobbing my heart out. My parents were both in the room and were trying to calm me but I was having none of it. I knew it was right, I just didn't know how. I just knew it meant that he wouldn't be there anymore, which to me was not an option, so I didn't think about it. I clung to him and wouldn't let go. Mum tried desperately to get me to let go of him, but Dad told her to leave me be and I hugged myself to him, sobbing until I fell asleep.

Mum had a friend named Jean who owned the local paper shop. One Sunday she visited Mum and offered to have us to stay with her overnight, as they knew it would not be much longer until he passed. She was worried about us children being in the house. We were all packed off to stay at Jean's house, so that Mum could have peace and quiet while caring for Dad in his last hours. It was so difficult for her, caring for four children every day, with a sick husband, and she was only thirty-three.

While my brothers and I were safely tucked in at Jean's, my Nan and Granddad were with my Mum and Dad. Mum rested by his side in the chair, as she did every night. She had hardly slept properly during the previous six months, and she was tired, so very tired. Dad woke up and told her to lie down on the sofa to get some sleep, as she'd been awake continuously for almost twenty-four hours. She was hesitant, but he insisted, so she moved to the sofa and tried to read, to keep awake and watch over him. But for the first time in many nights she fell into a deep sleep.

She woke suddenly, disorientated; it was so quiet - no heavy breathing. She knew he was gone. Fear consumed her. Trying to calm her panic and draw her strength, she noticed how the room was cold and silent; sorrow gripped her but she knew she had to face this. She sat up and opened her eyes.

Many years later she told me all this and said she was so angry. She wanted to be with him by his side, telling him he was loved whether he could hear it or not, as he passed. Dad must have known the time was close and he didn't want to hurt her any more. Mum later realised that when she awoke the blanket she had covered herself with had been removed from her and was folded neatly and placed on his chair. To this day she has no idea how it got there.

The next day I went to school from Jean's house. Nothing seemed out of place to me, but it was the day my life would change forever. I was collected by the Headmistress at about ten o'clock and taken to her office. I was wondering what I'd done wrong now. As I walked in I saw Mum was waiting for me. She had been crying and her eyes were red. She was very composed as she quietly and calmly explained to me that Dad had gone, he had died. He had become very poorly and he had to leave, but he would be watching over me. I couldn't understand what she was saying initially. Of course he hadn't gone - how could he go? My brain would not process the information. It was like the earth beneath my feet started to disappear and I was falling… it felt bad, very bad. I will never forget the feeling of heaviness in my chest.

I was aware of being steered out of the school to go home, and I remember telling my Mum that I had to see him. I had a desperate physical need to see him. When we got to the house my grandparents were there. Mum told them what I wanted and with Granddad by my side she led me into the lounge. I was scared, I don't know why. She slowly led me to the bed. Dad was covered with a white cotton sheet. As she pulled it back, my eyes drifted onto his face and I screamed! Who was that? He was grey, not like my Daddy at all. I collapsed, sobbing uncontrollably. My Granddad scooped me up, took me in his arms and brought me upstairs to the front bedroom to try to soothe me and explain to me what had happened and that everything was all right. I cried with a fierceness that I didn't repeat for many years afterwards. I sat and stared from the window; it was then that I saw an ambulance arrive. I knew they were going to take him away. My mind uttered a silent plea, "Please don't take him away"; he was my all, my life. My fists banged against the windows as I was screaming, "Stop! Don't take him away!" I was in panic and very angry; it felt like such a betrayal. I didn't understand why they were taking him. Where were they taking him? All I knew was that he was leaving me and I didn't want him to go. How could anyone explain this in words that would heal or make any sense to a six year old? I was desolate, destroyed. I wanted to die too.

My life went hazy over the following few days. Mum told me it was best that I didn't attend his funeral because I was too young and I didn't really understand. I understood enough! That was very wrong. Surely you should always be given the choice, no matter what your age. I knew that it had happened, but apart from my dream no-one had told me it was going to happen. It was from this point that my trust in anyone went flying out of the window. I felt betrayed and alone.

Every night for quite a while afterwards I cried for my Dad. I missed him so much. A child's pain is so hard to articulate and parents sometimes do not notice, wrapped up in their own pain. In the year after that, I rarely smiled. No-one talked about it. Mum had to carry on as normal, to keep us all fed and clothed, but not me. I couldn't carry on like before. I had changed. I would not eat and I lost weight. I wanted my Daddy back - he was my life. I used to talk to Mum and cry that I wanted him back, but she would cry too and that made me feel awful so I stopped talking to her. I would crawl into her bed, on his side; I didn't want to be alone at night, the dark scared me. I became withdrawn and nervous, scared of everything and everyone.

Then, quite out of the blue, I developed a stutter. This was to become the enduring bane of my life. It was terrible and resulted in many years of humiliation, including at the hands of certain teachers at school. They thought it was hilarious to get me to say my name when I physically couldn't. One teacher in particular did not understand that I couldn't control it, and kept saying, "Just say your name" when I could not without stuttering. They made me do it again and again, in front of the whole class, everyone laughing and giggling at me – it was complete humiliation day after day, added to the heavy burden of sorrow that I was carrying around with me.

Conversation about Dad with my brothers, too, was very limited. They hardly mentioned him. We just didn't discuss it much. It was a painful episode for all of us, and we all suffered in our own ways. Sometimes, when I would try talking to them about him, they would shrug it off, obviously too painful.

I spent a lot of time with them. I became 'one of the boys' and they treated me as such. No-one could ever get me in a dress. Mum despaired of me, her little girl, her Jacqueline. I thought it was horrific to be treated any differently. I would sneak upstairs to their bedroom at night when I was supposed to be asleep. I was forever being scolded, but I would just rather be with them. I was closest to Andy, and he is now the only brother I have on this side of life. I have loved my Dad every day since he left this Earth. It is now more than forty-three years since he passed and each year in May I email Andy, just the date… "I know," he always replies.

When I think back now to how Mum coped, she was amazing. Money was so tight she had no option other than to start working, and my wonderful grandparents would come to the house daily when we came home from school to help care for us while Mum was at work. Life continued but Mum found it very hard. Finances were strained with such a large family so she rented a room in the house to a lodger - I thought he was wonderful and he was a great support to all of us, like one of the family. I would creep into his room and curl up on the bottom of his bed to sleep while he was working. He never said much, just looked at me and nodded his assent. I felt safe there with someone watching over me. I suppose he took over the authority role for all of us and I remember him being very strict - we were all a bit scared of him when he shouted. But he was always kind to me and I was really upset when he left us.

Painful

Life is sometimes painful,
too much to bear, it seems.
Those times I find it best to live
wrapped up in my dreams.

—RAY EDWARDS

CHAPTER TWO

Change

I started hearing noises and seeing strange things around the time that my Mum remarried. I was eight years old and not happy about it at all. I didn't want anyone to replace my Dad, not ever.

Mum was beautiful and very young to be widowed, so it wasn't surprising that she would find someone else. Even I could tell that she loved Ernie, though at the time I thought she was being a traitor to my father. I was not going to let her get married without knowing how I felt, but I didn't know how to put what I wanted to say into words. So I took action.

On the day of their wedding, I didn't smile at all for the whole day and was deliberately miserable. I have the photos to prove it! I was a bridesmaid and wore a similar dress to Mum's. My hair was set in curls with a velvet headband and I looked sweet and cute - but sullen, boorish and mean. How could anyone replace my Dad? I felt incredibly bitter, sad and angry, and it was the only way I could express my pain. I didn't tell anyone this, but how could they not know? Was it only me? I just didn't get it. How could these people act like they were happy? Even though it was two years after Dad's death, that was no time to me.

Mum was sad about my behaviour which made me glad, because it meant she knew how I felt. Having the freedom to make judgements is a luxury granted to children. But I feel bad about it now; I couldn't know then what she knew, or have to face what she faced. And I don't blame her in any way for all that ensued.

Then it all began...

Six months after the wedding, I started hearing strange sounds and seeing strange people in the house. I was eight years old and I cannot put into words how utterly terrified I was. I understand these things now but, as a child, how could I explain to people so they'd understand? So they'd believe me? Unless people have had such experiences, they either can't or don't want to know. When you first become aware of the 'spookies' visiting, it can get very scary even for an adult.

I distinctly remember a conversation that happened just before the strange events. My brothers and I, with Mum and stepdad Ernie, were on holiday in Kent to see Ernie's family. It was a good holiday with lots of sunshine and playing on the beach, and it was good to get away. We went to visit his brother, John, who was a very animated man and completely different to my Dad. I liked him, he was funny. One evening we all went to a pub and he bought us crisps and fizzy pop as we sat and listened to him relate a ghostly experience he had had the previous week. I remember thinking to myself, 'A ghost... what's a ghost?' He explained it as someone who is dead but comes back here. 'Oh,' I thought, 'can they do that?' It sounded scary, so I put it out of my mind.

Then a couple of nights after we returned home, I was awoken suddenly by my bed shaking, moving with an unseen force. At first I thought it might have been one of my brothers playing a trick on me, but then I saw shadows walking around the room, clearly visible in the dim light that glowed through my curtains. I was terrified. Then the noises started, splitting the night silence loudly - someone was rasping for breath, and unearthly footsteps the like of which you have never heard, in the hallway and onto the stairs, climbing slowly, rhythmically, one step at a time...

I thought, 'Are these the ghosts?' Every single night without fail I would be woken between 2 and 4 a.m. I could clearly hear them downstairs, my hearing spiked to perfection, as if I were in the same room.

My bedroom was on the first floor at the back of the house, directly above the dining room which led out to the garden through a metal door, and whenever the key was turned I could hear it quite clearly. It was usually a familiar and comforting sound, someone being awake downstairs and guarding the house; I could sleep in peace because I was convinced 'they' would not come around when people were up and about. But this key, in the dead of night, would be turning and turning - like someone was locking and unlocking the door. It was clear and precise. Then the door to the lounge would bang downstairs. Whoever it was did not do quiet - they wanted to be heard.

The most frightening experience was of someone sitting on my bed and shaking me awake. It was a single bed flush against the wall and – no ambiguity here – I clearly felt the bed dip down under their weight. As soon as I found the courage to move, which took me a while, and steel myself to turn the light on, it stopped. I would put my fingers in my ears and hum to myself because I didn't want to hear people walking around the house in the dead of night. Yet out of the silence someone was stamping across the landing, time after time, and doors were opening and closing. The bathroom light was on a pull string and this would make the sound of being turned on and off; I even saw the light under the gap in my door. But I heard no-one else moving around in the other bedrooms of the house, only mine, only ever mine.

It happened every single night with no respite. I would dread going to bed because I knew what was going to happen, but I was made to go at the same time every evening and off would go the lights. "There's nothing there," my mother would reply when I said I was terrified of the dark. No, not terrified, that doesn't even come close! I always tried to leave the light on, but it would be turned off by Mum or Ernie. I lay in bed crying, begging for it to stop, wishing someone else in the house would wake up so it would stop.

I didn't experience so much during the day but there would be strange occurrences, objects moving and doors opening before I walked through them. Could my life could get any worse? My stutter got worse. I could barely say one word after another. I did try to tell Mum about the noises and the other experiences but she would say, "Don't be silly" or "You imagined it" or even "It's just the house settling", not even contemplating that they could be real. For many people in those days, things like that just didn't happen; it was not in the media spotlight like it is these days. Back then it was 'out of sight, out of mind'. I just didn't know what to think because when you're that age you completely rely on adults telling the truth; you believe they're telling you the truth, and in their minds they were. Only now does my Mum know different.

She did start to leave her bedroom door open at night, so that she could hear the noises too, but no-one else heard them. It was just me. I used to sit and wonder if there was something wrong with me. Some-one hated me, or I'd done something very wrong to deserve this. What was it? I tried to discuss it with my friends, but learned to shut up very quickly when they looked at me 'that' way. I told some of my teachers about it. They were kind and listened to me but all they said was, "Have you told your parents?" The looks they gave me - they didn't believe me, it was pointless. I was completely stuck, with no-one to talk to, with continuous wide-eyed fear. I just had to put up with it.

Eventually, because of my constant unhappiness, Mum decided to take me to see a doctor. He questioned me thoroughly about what was happening and I told him everything truthfully. After the session he told Mum that there was nothing wrong with me and that I would grow out of it. I was both relieved and cross at the same time, and said to Mum, "See? I told you so!" Maybe the doctor just thought I was a little strange - a lot of people did. So I hid within myself, kept my head down, did my best to cope and eventually stopped saying anything to anyone, because no-one else could see what I was seeing or hear what I was hearing. Why was I the only one? I just prayed that it would eventually go away.

Salvation came in the form of my beautiful maternal grandmother, Gladys. She believed me, and I will love her forever for that. She gave me hope.

My Granddad was such a warm, funny and kind man. I used to sit on his lap while he held his breath until his face turned pink. I found it hilarious. He used to laugh too and his teeth would drop down, so he'd hurriedly push them back, feigning embarrassment. Nan was a very fussy lady. She was always busy and it seemed like she was everywhere at once, bustling about in her pinafore, running a ship-shape home. She was always talking about ships and used to say to me, "One day if you're lucky, your ship will come in and you'll have all you need."

Granddad died suddenly in 1975. He'd gone into hospital as he wasn't well, and I was told he would be out shortly - but he just died. I was twelve years old and asked myself, "Why do they keep leaving me?" I cried so many tears. It felt like it was something to do with me. Nan moved in with us and slept with me in my bedroom. I never minded sharing with her; she was great company and I loved her dearly as she'd always been there for me when my Mum couldn't be. I also felt I would be safer with her in the room. Surely 'they' would not be so noisy with her there? How wrong that was! Unfortunately, if you're not meant to hear the spirit world then you won't no matter what you do. Some experiences are meant for you and some are not.

I don't know why, but I never woke her up when the noises started. Maybe I should have but I didn't want to hear "Don't be silly" again. I wanted so much to wake her, to have her hold me, to tell me it would be all right and that she could hear them too and it was all real. Grand-mother just slept soundly on. So it continued as before.

But then one night things came to a head and she did wake up. My frightened, glaring eyes stared at her and her face said it all. I saw initial shock, disbelief, then a knowing look on her face - did she understand? She looked at my feeble form, threw back the covers of her bed and hurried over to me, grabbing me in a protective hug. "Don't worry," she said, "they won't hurt you." I collapsed sobbing with relief into her nightdress and she rocked me and stroked my head with soothing words of comfort. At last I wasn't alone.

I believe my grandmother had some connection to the spirit world in the same way that I had. She did tell me a few times that she saw Granddad looking at her in the night. That cheered me up immensely. "So, you too!" I thought. She was such a kind, loving woman and always understood and tolerated me, and never judged me. She didn't think that I just had 'a vivid imagination'. She believed me and gave me hope.

When I was twelve years old, we were all sitting in the living room around the television watching The Muppet Show. It was a Sunday evening. I remember the details vividly and this experience will always be indelibly etched on my mind, as it was the first time I saw true evidence of the spirit world.

It was winter and dark outside, quite early in the evening. I was wearing purple trousers with an orange motif on them. I was fiddling and pulled the motif off, leaving a big hole in the trousers; I have no idea why I did things like that. Mum saw me do it and was furious with me, sending me straight upstairs to bed as a punishment. I didn't want to go, it was dark, but refusing was not an option. At least the landing light was on though, and it shone a glow through into my bedroom. Then suddenly all the lights went off. I knew this was part of the punishment, as Ernie knew how much I was scared of complete darkness. I sat in my room, hoping and praying that I wouldn't hear any noises. After a few minutes, feeling brave, I crept out to go and switch on the landing light but Ernie was waiting there, hiding to see if I would try to escape my punishment. He shouted at me to get back into my room and keep the lights off, so I ran back inside. How I hated him!

I waited, straining my ears until I heard the living room door click shut downstairs, then crept out onto the landing again and gingerly looked down the stairs ... I stood there rigid with fear and disbelief as I saw my grandfather standing at the bottom of the stairs, looking up at me with an affectionate smile on his face. I had never been so shocked. Completely spooked, I was riveted to the spot! He glowed with a soft, golden light around him illuminating his whole body very clearly. I could see his clothes, his face and his loving smile. He was completely solid as if still physical, his cardigan hanging around him as it always did, wearing his old slippers. His eyes were the same. All his features were as I knew him.

There were so many sudden and conflicting feelings, it was over-whelming. My eyes were wide, my mouth was dry. Although I was scared, there was nothing scary about him – but he shouldn't be there. Just his being there was scary. I could not reason this. My heart was in my mouth and I wanted to be sick. I panicked and ran, jumped back into bed as fast as I could, hid under the blankets and burst into tears. It was almost as though I passed out; I slept deeply until Mum woke me three hours later for supper. I tried to tell her what I saw, but again she said that I must have imagined it.

So, I thought, maybe it was my grandfather and not my Dad who was visiting me at night? Or maybe it was both? Oh great, both of them! And so it continued, night after night.

The summers seemed so much longer and hotter when I was a child and children were expected to play outside most of the day. My brothers and I always played boys' games together, climbing over fences, leaping off the shed roof and always getting told off for it. I was treated like one of the boys. It was about this time that my name became Jac or Jacqui, never Jacqueline. I refused to answer to that. Only my Dad could call me that and he wasn't here anymore, so Jacqueline no longer existed.

In those days, it wasn't a problem if you went out to play and didn't tell anyone where you were going. Around this time I started to go to the churchyard, to Dad's grave. I would always go on my own, sneaking away and never telling anyone; it was my secret. In the winter it was a very stark place, but in the summer it was beautiful, with the pungent aromas of many trees and flowers. His grave is at the rear of the churchyard and it was one of the first in a new section. I could lie down on the grass and not be seen, and believe he was with me. I felt closer to him there and was completely hidden from prying eyes by the lines of graves in front of his. I felt so much peace there and used to spend hours making daisy chains and talking to him. It just seemed completely natural to me.

These days, there's a plethora of TV shows and films about spirit, so it's not a taboo subject anymore. But back then, everyone I met seemed to think that if you can't see it and you can't touch it, then it doesn't exist. My parents' generation said, "It's just your imagination" as an explanation for anything strange because they couldn't relate to it. We mustn't judge the past and the people in it by what we know now. We are where we are now because of the past – it has its purpose and its meaning.

But now, I think the worst thing that a parent can say to a child in my kind of situation is, "I don't believe you." I really wish my Mum had sat down with me and talked to me about it, or just listened to what I was saying even if she didn't believe me. Offloading my fears would have really helped me. In my work today, I have many calls from parents asking for help in talking to their young children who are experiencing what I did - albeit not to the same degree. It is sad to find that parents are still scared. So much fear, and for what benefit?

Please listen to your children if they come to you with stories like this. Children are closer to the spirit world, so they will always feel much more. Be patient, comfort them and tell them they are in control; they can tell the 'spooky' to leave at any point and they will listen. Tell children they can choose. Help them to understand that spirits are not evil or scary, but are very loving. More than likely a spirit is someone close, wanting to watch over and care for the child.

CHAPTER THREE

Anger

*A feeling started to grow inside me, not so much of fear but of
anger. Something snapped within me. I was really angry!
I flung off the blankets and got up thinking,
'You have GOT to be kidding me!'*

On my thirteenth birthday, everything changed again. The previous
year I had been given my own room. It was a small single room at the
front of the house, decorated with blue flowered wallpaper. It felt
lighter and less imposing than the bedroom I had slept in with my
grandmother. She was now on the lower floor of the house, having had
a serious operation. Graham, my eldest brother, had moved into my old
room and always slept like a baby. That annoyed me - how could he?

I was still being woken every night. I discovered that ear plugs do
absolutely nothing. You can still hear spirits, whether you are wearing
them or not. The night before my thirteenth birthday I was quite
excited about becoming a teenager and went to sleep quickly. But then
my eyes were suddenly open and I was wide awake. Glancing at the
clock, it was 4.20 a.m. Footsteps on the stairs – oh, here we go again.
That noise! This time it was louder and stronger than before and there
were three parts to it: a stomp, a breath and an 'Aaaah' sound. I lay and
listened to my heart pumping on my ribs, as it always did. I had put up
with this for so long, night after night, and now a new feeling started to
grow inside me, not so much of fear, but of anger. Something snapped

within me. I was angry, really angry! I flung the blankets off and got up, thinking 'You have GOT to be kidding me!'

It had been a constant form of torture to me for so long that my anger made me brave. I stamped across the room to the door, back to the curtains and back again, hoping 'they' would hear me and go away. All the time I was talking to myself, steeling myself. I placed my hand on the door handle with every intention of flinging it open, but I was frozen to the spot and just couldn't. I could hear the footsteps getting closer to the top of the stairs, nearly the thirteenth step, nearly at the top. I knew those stairs so well, I always counted them, and each one had its own creaky floorboard. Then I stepped back from the door and angrily shouted, "Stop! That's enough!" It was loud enough for everyone in the house to hear me, no matter where they were.

The footsteps stopped instantly. I couldn't believe it - complete silence. I was stunned. I waited for them to begin again - still silence. I climbed back into bed and lay there listening. I'd been forceful, I'd meant every word, I'd told them to stop and they stopped! How did that happen? Why hadn't I realised this before… and why now? I felt powerful and strong for a change and from that moment onwards the change was tangible. I had made a stand and I felt proud.

I started to sleep better after that night, and felt better in myself because somehow I had made the noises stop. And I was relieved and grateful that I was no longer tortured by the nightly routine that had dominated my life for so long. But although I felt in control, I still had so many questions to ask. Why? Who? How? I didn't know who to ask, or how to take it any further. I decided that probably the footsteps on the stairs belonged to my Dad because the awful strained breathing that went with them was similar to the way he sounded when he was very poorly and slept downstairs. It was a sound that everyone could hear, all over the house. In a way there was a certain comfort for me, feeling Dad close by.

This was a turning point. The spookiness was nowhere near as scary as it had been. The noises were fainter and muffled, light footsteps, nothing else. I would still hear people walking around the house, sometimes things would disappear or move from place to place, and people would sit on my bed - but I had always had that. Doors would still occasionally open before I went through them. That has always happened to me. I knew someone was doing it, I could feel them. But only now did it occur to me that they could hear me as much as I could hear them, and that made a real difference. We began to communicate in some way. Whoever it was, I hoped they would stay unseen now and quiet. They could come around me as much as they liked when I was sleeping, but not wake me up. If I could ignore them, hopefully they would ignore me. As to what had happened before… we would just forget it, I could live with that.

My brothers and I chatted about this from time to time. They didn't seem to believe me and I didn't find out until many years later that they had heard similar noises, though nowhere near as much. As I got older, it was sometimes hard to distinguish a drunken brother crawling up the stairs trying to find his bedroom from an errant spookie trying to make their presence felt. It was amusing, as if they were laughing with me. An understanding somehow grew within me - there was a place where they were, and a place where I was. I knew of their presence and they knew of mine, and we resided in a kind of symbiosis - each their own separate part, but actually one.

This period of my life was dominated by unseen forces that I perceived to be out of this world. I believed I was being picked on, singled out. Why couldn't Mum hear anything?[1] What about when I saw my Granddad - how was that possible? He was as solid as you or me. My questions went unexplained for a long time and I still don't understand completely. Maybe I only will when I go over to the spiritual plane; after all, we don't have to know everything. No-one I asked did actually explain or understand.

Yet I knew that all I had gone through was real. My grandmother had experienced it with me. Could there be something here that people didn't know about? Was there something much more than we allowed ourselves to know? Was it because we are afraid to ask? Was I the only who experienced this? Indeed, no-one else ever told me that they

---

[1] She told me years later that she would walk around the house at night looking for my Dad and asking him to come back to her, just once. I still find that so sad, as I now know he was there all the time.

experienced phenomena like I did, so I just kept quiet. I was really fed up with people looking at me like I had three heads and came from Venus. I just wished that someone would show me something to answer my questions. Was that too simplistic?

I did go to church over the years, and the thought of an ever-present God or spirit watching over me was comforting. But I didn't dare ask anyone there. I knew they would think I was a devil child. All I seem to remember from Sunday School was that Jesus wanted me for a sunbeam, apparently.

Religion is taught from books. It informs us of what we need to find and what to believe within that teaching. We learn what we are taught. So what if there is something else that doesn't fit with that teaching, that doesn't resonate with us - should we just ignore it? Is it something different? Maybe it is not the religion itself that's the problem but the people who condition us with what they believe. I listened when I went to church, searching for some explanation, but what I heard did not fit with what I had experienced.

How I disliked Ernie. Again and again we would argue, or rather he shouted and I listened. He scared me. I couldn't answer back - not allowed to, more than my life was worth. He said "No" for no other reason that he could. If I only wanted to stay out for another half an hour, what was it to him? Oh, I forgot, we had to do as he said. But who gave him that power? I wished he would just leave me alone.

I didn't achieve much at school. I disliked it intensely. How could you enjoy a place where you could not be yourself but just had to fit in with others? I was teased over my stutter and couldn't wait to leave. I just wanted to do my own thing, not that I knew quite what that was. However, I did learn how to be a chameleon, changing my colours to fit situations and people and behaving as people expected me to. Sometimes you have to conform; not that I like that, I never have.

So I continued in the same way, stuttering through my teenage years until I was eighteen, when I had my next bereavement. By this time I was working in a polytechnic kitchen. My beautiful Nan died after a stroke in 1981. I went to see her in hospital and I knew she was near to passing. She knew it too, so I sat with her and held her hand. I loved her very much; she had always been there for me, defended me and loved me. I can still remember my Mum's cries when she received the 'phone call in the early hours of the morning. We all woke up early that day. This time I didn't cry. I don't know why. Maybe I knew she couldn't live here any longer without suffering and I don't like to see anyone suffer. Although she was dying, on some level I knew it would be all right. We had that special bond. We all had a strong relationship with her and missed her chats - she could talk the hind legs off a donkey (that must be where I get it from). I will always be grateful for her kindness, her love and support for me in the darkest of nights, for speaking up for me when no-one believed me. I know she will always be watching over me.

A week after she died, just after New Year, I was in the car with my brother Andy and my boyfriend Pete (who went on to be my husband). We'd been out and on returning home realised we were out of cigarettes so decided to drive to a twenty-four hour garage to get some. It was raining hard and there was a lot of water sitting on the road. As we drove into a sharp bend the car skidded, aquaplaned, hit a bridge made of long metal railings and then dropped over the bridge - twelve feet straight down.

How we survived that night I shall never know. There had been many accidents at that bridge in the past, and afterwards the police told us that no-one had survived before as the cars always rolled over. By some miracle ours had not. A metal bar from the bridge had entered through the passenger door, missed me by a hair's breadth and turned into the car floor, swung us around and dropped us like a stone onto the grass a few feet from the river. We were very lucky; it could have been the end for us all. When the car eventually stopped moving and crashing - it all seemed to happen in slow motion - I turned to look for Andy. The back seat was split in two and the window was gone. I screamed for him in panic, then heard him shout, "I'm ok" – he'd landed in the only pile of horse manure in the field and it saved him, cushioning his fall as he was thrown from the car, out of the back window. He was bruised and scratched, but besides smelling bad he was fine. I escaped with a cut on my chin and I remember chewing on glass.

I was still sitting in the passenger seat when Pete jumped out of the car and climbed back up onto the road. He tried to flag down a car and three cars passed him before someone stopped. I was in shock and shaking, and I felt sick. I remember a policeman saying to me, "You were very lucky to survive this. Someone must have been looking after you - they must want you for something." Little did he know…

At that exact time my stepdad Ernie was listening to the CB radio in his car. Afterwards he said, "I just knew it was you." He came racing down to us and was one of the first on the scene.

We had a very troubled relationship. I was expected to call him 'Dad' which I found very hard. That said, over time I found a place for him to be who he was in my life, though it took a long time to get there. He was a very strict man who'd been brought up that way and only seemed to know the tough way. Our relationship was strained from day one. I think the problem was that he just didn't know how to handle raising a girl, especially one like me who didn't trust him at all. He was more tolerant with my brothers, though misbehave and the belt would come out; that was always a great leveller. He'd been married, with two sons, when he met Mum and got divorced to marry her. Soon afterwards he legally adopted us all and we changed our surnames. Mum told me years later that she did it to protect us because there was a certain prejudice towards children who had a different name to their parents. That's just how it was back then, and she did it with the best of intentions. But did that make it right? Did it really matter what people thought? I was eight years old and not at all happy. It was as if I'd never had another Dad.

Ernie would shout and I would react. He scared me. Physically he was very tall with dark eyes and could be quite imposing. He'd been raised in a very strict environment and was in the RAF during the war. There were many battles over the years, usually with him trying to force his ways on me. Didn't he realise that was never going to work? I was rarely allowed out at night until I was sixteen and even then had to be home by ten o'clock, although my brothers were allowed out much later. Boys loomed for me… I was quite sheltered and innocent, but when I did go out - oh my, the freedom was great and I did enjoy myself!

On my eighteenth birthday I was taken out by a group of friends with my brother Andy and Pete, who had arranged a bit of a get-together for me as a surprise. I had a great night and completely lost track of the time. It was after midnight and I went into a panic because I knew Ernie was going to go ballistic when I went home. Andy told me not to worry as he would sort it for me. I somehow doubted that – I'd always had to deal with it myself. As I opened the front door of the house to creep in, Ernie was standing ominously at the top of the staircase, looking so angry his eyes were burning and his mouth was fixed in a straight line. Mum was peering over the banister, a strained and concerned look on her face. I pulled myself up to my full five feet tall and told him I was now old enough to take care of myself, there was no need for this and he should stop now. Ernie slowly descended the stairs. I backed away and Andy moved to stand in front of me. He said to Ernie, "You'll have to go through me to get to her." Never had any of my brothers stood up for me before, and I was so grateful. Ernie stilled as he reached the hallway and stood in front of Andy, glaring at us both. I held my breath… then he turned, walked silently back upstairs and went to bed. Following that evening he did his usual thing of not talking to me for months. It was a bit of a relief really.

All that said, he did love my Mum and she loved him, though for many years she was in the middle of constant fights and arguments. We were a volatile lot. Indeed, I thought she would never admit how mean he was to me, but she did eventually. I only ever truly forgave him when he passed to the spirit world.

Throughout most of his life he was a very fit man, but when he retired he became very immobile and would just seem to sit all day and sleep, becoming weaker year by year. My Mum is a young at heart soul, always wanting to be busy, so he would let her do what she wanted and he was happy just by himself. In his later years he developed a degenerative pulmonary disease and, when he reached eighty, he became very old, very fast. He would sit in his chair in the sitting room and not move for most of the day, just watching TV. Not long after that he suffered a stroke, which affected his bad moods even more. I started to temper my feelings for him a little. He was just a sad old man.

Ernie had absolutely no belief in the spirit world, and thought it was 'a load of rubbish'. One afternoon, as usual, he was sitting in the lounge with the TV on, checking the horses that he'd bet on that day in the newspaper. Without warning the TV went quiet and the screen went blank. Suddenly on the screen appeared a photograph of my brother Graham (who had died by then); it stayed there for a good few seconds, then the picture returned to the racing. It really shook him up. I did have a chuckle. He was adamant in denying what he'd seen, never wanted to believe anything to do with the spooky side of life and would smirk when I talked of it. But I knew more than him on this subject; it was the only thing I did know that I was good at in life. He was terrified of dying, which is one reason why he didn't want to acknowledge it.

CHAPTER FOUR

Is it Really Love?

He loves me… he loves me not… he loves me…
Nope, he definitely doesn't!

Up to my early thirties, my life had contained so many low points. I just seemed to swing from one bad situation to another. But I cared about people, maybe too much. To love, to care and to listen you need compassion, which develops when you experience life. It is brought to you by the people around you and the experiences you have. It is about receiving love and assistance from someone who has travelled the same road. To receive the love through life's lessons takes time.

Growing up from thirteen was very difficult, particularly at secondary school. I was a good girl at school and kept close to the people I knew, but my stutter was terrible. I couldn't say more than a couple of words, and people can be so cruel. (Remembering this handicap makes it all the more unbelievable that I can now stand and speak in public.) I never had any help with this affliction and it took a long time to get a handle on it. So I disliked school intensely. I was not an academic, but I did love History and English. However I consider myself lucky that I had some lovely friends. There were about six of us girls who always used to hang out together.

I was never so happy as when I could leave school and get out into the big wide world. I wanted to spread my wings. I mean, how hard could it be? I've always been too eager to go where angels fear to tread. At seventeen I met my future husband, Pete. He was so much fun - tall, handsome and blond, and I adored him. He was a musician and a very, very good guitarist. We would meet with a group of regular friends every day; we all knew each other extremely well and spent a lot of time together. It was around then that I also met my best friend, who was introduced as Tob and was standing by a pool table with a cigarette in his mouth, a pint in one hand a pool cue in the other. He wore jeans, a denim jacket that smelled of patchouli, and had a smile that made his eyes squint. He was, and is, the kindest and nicest man you will ever meet on God's green Earth. He became my protector and saviour, and little did I know we would be friends all my life.

We had a great time filled with laughter, lots of loving and fun. Everyone knew how difficult it was for me at home. This was no secret. After a year of being with Pete, we split up – the grass was greener, that sort of excuse – but reunited two weeks later. How could I not? I loved him very much. Ernie didn't speak to me for many months because of this, and Pete wasn't allowed in the house at all. He would collect me from outside. It got to the point that I'd had enough of being the villain and there were constant rows at home.

Then at eighteen I was offered a job at a country pub, living close by, so I gathered up the small amount of my possessions and moved out, not looking back. Mum said to me, "So you're really going then?" Oh yes! I had to because I couldn't stand the atmosphere in the house anymore, so oppressive and heavy, with everyone walking on eggshells. I always felt like I was at fault. So I decided that if I moved everyone would be a lot happier and I could have some peace. It really was that simple.

Pete and I were married a month before my twentieth birthday. He was twenty-one. Not everyone approved, for obvious reasons I think, but Mum was great and helped as much as she could. The wedding day was amazing and yielded my favourite photograph, which sits on the shelf in my lounge today, of me with my three brothers when we were all so young. I had three beautiful bridesmaids, dressed in purple.

I dressed for the day alone, slipping on the beautiful white dress Mum had bought for me. It was a cloudy October morning as I sat on the stool in my bedroom putting on just a little make-up, staring at my reflection and thinking about my Dad, wishing he were there. It was then I heard a very audible voice, telling me that I would be divorced in two years. It was calm and quiet, just imparting information. It shook me! Somehow that voice was familiar, and I knew I'd heard it before. But what should I do? There was an hour to go. I now understand that voice; he comes to me when I need him, although I don't know that I need him! He's the same man who told me, in my dream as a child, that my Dad was going to die.

Now, the fact that we hear does not mean that we always listen, but oh how we should! We are human, that's the problem. We don't take any notice of the little voice in our head. So I did nothing, said nothing, put it out of my mind and was married. It was a fun day and at the end I took my bouquet and placed it on Dad's grave. It was dusk and cold as I stood there, hugged my arms around myself, whispered "I love you, Daddy" and turned away with tears in my eyes to live another chapter of my life without him.

A few days before the wedding, I had been at Pete's parents' house, looking out of the beautiful picture window in the lounge at the wonderful views over the countryside. I looked up and Fred, Pete's father, was standing at my side. He smiled and handed me a package wrapped in tissue paper. Inside, in a beautiful frame, was a picture of my Dad. At that time I only had one picture of him. Fred had obtained it somehow and had it enlarged. I will never forget that and have never been so touched by such simple kindness. I still have that picture, to this day. It sits on the windowsill in my bedroom and watches over me.

We had a wonderful honeymoon in the south of France. Then reality hit. When we returned home we lived with his parents. They were wonderful to us, the loveliest and best of people, but I always felt out of place there. It was as if I did not belong. Pete would tell me not to be so self-conscious, but that was just the way I felt. I just never felt good enough and, to be honest, some of his family thought that too. Two months after getting married I found out that I was pregnant, somewhat of a surprise for both of us. We just had to try our best and get on with it, certainly not in the most favourable of circumstances. We didn't have many possessions, we had no work, no home, no money and we were still living at my in-laws.

But by some miracle of fate, or something else, Pete was offered a job in another town - an opportunity for a new life. We were eligible for social housing and we could try to begin a new pathway. It was very exciting. The house materialised quite quickly. Inside it was painted entirely in blue, just slapped on from top to bottom. Those blue walls drove me slightly crazy after a time, so I painted them white. We still had no furniture and no money to buy any, so it was the kindness of our families that helped us to put the basics into the house. And thank goodness for wedding presents or else we would have had nothing. Maybe I should have known that there was something ominous about this time because the number of the house was thirteen.

It was at this time that I met another life-long friend, named Sandie. She lived at number fifty and had a small son. We became great friends and I honestly don't know how I would have coped without her during my pregnancy. I was so sick all the time. She would feed me, care for me, and even let me stay there when Pete went to a party and forgot about me. I have never been as angry as I was that night, when he rolled in drunk! Elliott was born in 1984, a few months before I turned twenty-one. He didn't want to come into the world, and arrived only after a long labour. I had never been so tired in my life. But he was perfect and beautiful, the image of his father even then, and one of the two greatest joys in my life.

Now what was I supposed to do? There were no exams to take for parenthood so I just had to do the best I could. He became my reason for living, with his big blue eyes and blond hair. He would spend hours playing with cardboard boxes and loved watching washing machines!

Pete left very suddenly and that was his choice. He arrived home one evening and just wanted out of the marriage. I find it hard even now to say why, and I don't think he really knew. It certainly wasn't what I wanted. Neither of us was perfect, but we were learning and it takes time to figure out how to live with someone. We'd grown apart but we'd tried to make the best of it, and to be the best we could in the circumstances that surrounded us. He made it abundantly clear that he was going, though. He packed some clothes and walked out. I was bereft, shocked and numb. A week later he returned and wanted us to reunite but there was just no way I could ever do that. The trust was broken. He'd left me, he'd left his son. It hurt, but I could never go back. I'd learned from previous situations that it cannot be the same. Still, there's no point in pointing the finger of blame and I only hope that he found his happiness.

It was very difficult to manage in a strange town, with no family nearby and very few friends. I could have left and gone back home, but I saw that as defeat, and I was strong. I seem to have this inbuilt mechanism to survive, to prove something - but to whom? So I stayed with Elliott and did the best I could. With very little money, I had to make the choice on more than one occasion to feed Elliott or myself; it's sobering to know hunger. Sandie always came to my rescue, caring for Elliott when I went to work. I did whatever work I could find, mainly menial jobs, for quite a few years. Sometimes I did three jobs a day - cleaning in a bank from six to eight, working all day in an office, then cleaning in the evening from six to eight. That was tiring, but I would do anything for my son, he was my life.

At two years old Elliott went to a private nursery paid for by his father; he had the best we could give him and he thrived. He was quite a clever child and I poured all my love and energy into him. Later he would stay at my parents' house on alternate weekends and with Pete for the other weekend. Regardless of what we went through, it was only right that he did, and he loved his Daddy very much.

Then my life changed. During those difficult times I was exposed to people whom I would not otherwise have met and developed relationships I would never have experienced. Bear in mind I'd been exposed to very little of life. Before I knew it, I was married, had a child and then divorced within such a short space of time. It was all over in about two years. But from this point, boy, did I live! I had experiences that any sane person would not have put themselves through. I just got swept along with the charm and charisma and pulsing madness of situations, trusting everyone - what a lesson that was. I'd put all the bad stuff away in the back of my mind, into the 'Bad Experience' file. I should have put it in the 'Don't Do That Again' file, or the 'Beware, Men Will Hurt You If You Trust Them' file…

After this I had two very different relationships which spanned nearly three years. Both were very painful.

I loved the first man dearly, passionately and completely. He was tall, dark and very beautiful in every way. I fell hard! We were together for about eighteen months in total. He could be so romantic, leaving small notes around the house that would make me swoon. I'd never had that attention or those words said to me, and it blew me away. We had been together some months when he gave me a key to his home. I worked close by and the nursery was also near, so it made sense each day, after taking Elliott to nursery school, to dress at his place for work. It was his idea, I wouldn't have dreamed of asking. I was always taught that people who ask don't get.

One morning I arrived as usual and slipped my key into the lock. It didn't turn. Then the awful thought dawned that it was locked from the inside, which meant he was in. I felt a dread, a heavy pulling in my stomach. Something was wrong. I pressed the doorbell and hung on to it. When he opened the door he smiled and looked straight into my eyes and I knew he wasn't alone. I also knew instinctively who he was with, a woman who'd been chasing him for quite a while. I tried to climb the stairs but he dragged me into the lounge. Anger does not cover what I felt; I was burned by the pain. I left and sobbed all the way home, making my way to Sandie's house where I fell into her arms and she held me. I remember lying on her lounge floor and she sat with me while I wretched with sobs for hours. Everything had come crashing down and I had trusted the wrong man again. Why do I have endless hope and belief that everyone is essentially good?

This situation completely broke me at the time. I would never have believed I had that amount of passion, love, hate and anger all in one place. I was devastated, couldn't think straight, couldn't eat or sleep and didn't want to carry on with life. And to top it all someone invisible was following me around the house and I didn't know who it was. I could take no more, it was driving me mad.

One evening, I walked to the `phone box with Elliott and called Tob, hardly able to speak for the lump in my throat. I muttered, "I need you" and put the `phone down. I don't remember walking back or how long I was sitting there staring at the wall in the dark. He must have got into the car immediately and driven over, about a forty-five minute drive, and turned up with my brother Andy. They just packed me up and took me back to Leamington, where I stayed at Andy's house. Both he and his wife were so kind to me, let me come and go as I pleased, fed me and took care of me. They were wonderful. I also went to the graveyard and talked to my Dad, told him everything and felt much better. He could always do that for me, give me strength I didn't know I had.

I was never a quitter, so I went back to number thirteen. Immediately, I started to feel the spookies again, sensing them all around me. Someone was watching me all the time. Then strange occurrences started to happen in the house. There were noises. At one point I was worried about my sanity, but I knew there was something going on - something quite profound.

I had just asked my Dad for help again, so maybe it was him. It felt like someone was following me around the house. I would turn around and ask, "What? What do you want?" but I didn't get an answer. I didn't understand then that the little voice which spoke to me, cajoling and caring (and sometimes shouting) was my beautiful spirit friend. But I didn't know how to get answers. So much had happened since I was child, one tragedy after another, and I was so wrapped up in a world of drama and pain that I just couldn't hear. Pain blots out everything.

I hated being on my own so I seemed to fall into the second relationship. Many of us do that and live to regret it. Initially he was kind and attentive and helped me. For a while he took the responsibility away, so I could just be me and heal in a way that was bearable. But I learned very quickly that he was a very difficult man, bossy, domineering and mean. There is a fine line before relationships like this turn into something toxic. I did suffer emotionally and physically during that relationship. He was rough and he hurt me. He always made me feel it was my fault if he was angry, and I believed that I deserved all I was getting. I thought myself a really bad person. I became a possession and believed all the bad words fired at me. For a while I relinquished all my control, all my choices. I was scared, all the time. It's hard to explain to anyone who hasn't been through a situation like this how it happens.

I couldn't escape, I was just too afraid to try. But I had to end the relationship before something happened to one of us that could not be undone. Then one final evening he tried to pick on my son; I could have killed him that night and it galvanised me into action.

He left me thousands in debt and scared to death of people. At this point I could have retreated from the world, but I had my son who was my life, and that made me sit up and choose. I did try to stay there after this and make it on my own, but I knew it would be better to return and regroup, to start again at home. So in 1990 I moved back to live at my parents' house. That was very difficult. At the time I looked on at it as surrender and felt defeated. But I didn't see that I had any choice, since I couldn't make any more of a mess than I had already. Mum was happy to have me back. Elliott was now six years old and loved being with his grandparents. They would do anything for him and he wanted for nothing. Even Ernie developed a wonderful relationship with Elliott.

Mum had a lodger living at the house who'd been there some time. His name was Tom. He was Irish, warm, kind and funny. He asked me to go out with him on a date and I refused - I wasn't going there any-more! But he was brilliantly funny and disarming. Through being a friend, he lifted me out of the very dark place I'd found myself in. Slowly we began a relationship that then lasted five years, and which everyone encouraged. I was quite happy, went back to my usual slim self and enjoyed my life. Then after two years I was pregnant again. And again I was very sick almost from day one for about six months; I got bigger and bigger and more miserable.

I was only in hospital a short time and Thomas arrived in 1992. When I came back home with him space was minimal with three of us in a room. It was quite depressing. Then one day when I arrived home there was an envelope on the mat, an offer of a house not far away, again in social housing. I cried tears of relief. How on Earth did that happen? I thanked all the unseen forces for our good fortune. There were only two bedrooms and it was compact, but it was home for a while anyway.

The spookies were very prevalent in this house from the day I moved in, but somehow I didn't mind them being there. During my time in this house I started back onto the spiritual path, as I saw it. The fact is I had never left the path; it was rocky, but it was my path. I didn't know this at the time, but I learned so much through the pain and suffering; though how I got through all those years in one piece I don't know. I do know that I owe much to Tob, for without his daily love and support I would not still be here. I relied on him very heavily. We went to gigs together and he took care of me. What I owe him I could never repay with all the money in this world. We have a bond and an understanding that defies both time and space, even if not everyone understands it. It's a blessing to have a person like that in your life, someone who cares for you unconditionally.

Tom and I lived in that house for three years until our relationship became untenable and I ended it. He didn't want to be with me and I didn't want to be with him anymore. We had stayed together for Thomas, whom we both adored, but doing so made us both unhappy.

I said that I would never marry again – it was just too painful to contemplate, not a chance. But unbelievably, two months later, aged 33, I was married to my current husband. We had known each other some years before and were brought together again in the most unexpected way, at his mother's funeral. After that I met him by chance at my Mum's house, as he came to see her each week. He was amusing and strong, a real man and a confirmed bachelor!

We had been together a very short time when he asked me to marry him. Hey, who needs time when you know it's the right thing to do? And I just knew like I have never known anything so strongly in my life. I didn't even have to think about it, though I kept him waiting for a weekend. It was the best decision I ever made; he supports me totally, encourages me always and loves me completely. He's a private man, an honourable man.

When we got together he was away a lot with the Forces and I stayed home alone. I didn't mind that because I knew who I was marrying. Seventeen years later and I love him still. We both know who we are. My sons did clash with him initially, and that was hard for all of us. It didn't help that I would side with the boys every time; I was so protective of them and wouldn't listen when he told me to stand up and be firmer with them. I never could. My boys know I'm a complete pushover where they are concerned. He didn't have any children of his own and never wanted any, but he always supported them and helped them the best way he could.

I always see the positive side of things; I love everyone and give everyone the benefit of the doubt. My husband despairs of me, but we always talk. We may not always agree, but we always remember to keep open the channels of communication. It's so easy to let time pass by and become strangers, and I was never going to let that happen to us.

My husband doesn't share my enthusiasm for the spirit world in any way. There's no swaying him in his belief that when you're dead you're dead; but he supports me completely in everything I want to do and when I want to do it. It's funny how the circle has turned now; I am the one out and about and he stays at home. Without him I would never have had the courage to stand up and be the person I need to be. He encouraged me and hugged me when I didn't believe in myself - why should I when no-one had believed in me before? I owe him so much. He keeps me grounded, lets me know who I am and what is important, even if I sulk sometimes. At that time I found talking to people very hard and would avoid any socialising unless he was with me. No-one knew this. But I was learning, slowly, to fit myself into any scenario, not to be myself so much but to be what others expected. Now it's easier for me to act and to be someone I'm not.

I did wonder why I went through so much in so many short years, falling from one disaster to another. Now I know why, to help me to give to others and to say, "I know how you feel" - because I really do. I needed to go through those experiences to grow as a person. I had to experience difficult challenges, horrible situations and more emotional and physical pain than I would ever wish on anyone, in order to learn that it is transitory. Nothing ever stays the same, and the pain does not last. Eventually it subsides so that you can put it in a place where you can cope with it. All of this suffering created the person I am now.

And after all that - you know what? – I like the person I am now. If I met certain people from my past now, I honestly don't know what I would say. There is a lot I have forgiven, and there are also a few situations that I have not - but I'm still working on those. So look into yourself. Who are you now? What pain have you been through? Find it, acknowledge it, embrace it. Find yourself. Love yourself for all that you are and be all you can be right here, right now. You are more powerful that you realise. Everything you need is inside you, so look a little deeper...

Flame of love

I have known the pleasure,
I have known the pain,
I have wondered if my life
I could begin again.
The flame of love flares brightly,
When passion truly burns;
If we breathe upon its embers
Then, gently, warmth returns.

—RAY EDWARDS

CHAPTER FIVE

Graham

He had such blue eyes, but looked sad and so full of pain. If I could only end his suffering, I would. The tears he cried made me cry. I love him so much. Why do we suffer so much pain? Why do we choose this life? If only I could change it for him.

My brother Graham was the loveliest of men, the quietest and most thoughtful one of the four of us and he looked so much like my Dad. He was a simple man with a complicated life.

Graham became a Type One diabetic at sixteen, just as he was about to take his exams; it was the summer of 1976 and a really hot one. Mum had called the doctor for the second time because he was slipping into a coma; the doctor didn't wait for an ambulance but rushed him to hospital in his car. He learned to inject himself once a day, and I remember him practising on an orange with a needle. He hated being diabetic with a vengeance from the start, because this disease had totally ruined his future plans to join the RAF. He had always wanted to fly but it became clear quite quickly that he could no longer have a career in the services - they all refused his entry.

After a time he turned to the other gifts he had. He decided he wanted to work on car bodywork so he joined a large company and started his City and Guilds courses immediately. He really was a wonderful artist and had a real eye for colour and form, so easily passed all his qualifications. Then he started work for a company rebuilding

Austin Healeys and loved it; he had found one of his life's passions (the other would be his children).

He was happy at this time, particularly when the racing began; he loved speed and became a passenger in a car and bike outfit, racing around the country. That's where his troubles started. Each weekend he would travel, living out of the back of a truck with a group of friends. He drank a lot of alcohol. He just wanted to be part of all that scene, so he made his choice and had a ball. He was also heavily into CB radio and country and western music. He was popular, had a lot of friends and was just the nicest of men; a simple man who worked hard. He stopped racing when he got married as he thought it was unfair to have the responsibility of a family while risking his life each time he raced. Three children followed in quick succession, whom he adored. They really were everything to him and nothing was too much for his girls. It destroyed him when his wife left and took the children, without a word of warning. He went to work as usual one day and came home to an empty house. He was so shocked. That was the first time I had ever seen my brother cry and it broke my heart to see him in such pain. He did manage to find his children and spent time with them, as much as he could. But he was never really settled from that point and stumbled from one disaster to another.

In his mid-thirties more disaster struck. His kidneys ceased working and he became a renal patient having regular dialysis three times a week. It took hours each time. By Sunday night he was in agony with all the fluid in his body. We would visit where he was living and the lady who lived in the flat upstairs would tell us she'd been very worried about him as he'd been crying all the time. He was alone. That completely broke my heart. I had never seen anyone suffering from this condition before and it was hard to stand by and watch.

In 1997 Graham had a heart attack, 'luckily' just as he was leaving hospital after an appointment. It was due to a potassium overload and the machine at the hospital was broken so they couldn't test him at that time. He stayed in hospital for about three months and hated every second; all he could think about, and talk about, was escape. When I telephoned his doctor and asked for his prognosis on Graham, he was initially very careful with his words, skirting around the issue and general trying to be kind. I told him I wanted a direct approach, I had to know as I would be the one who would have to hold everyone together. He informed me that his arteries were that of an eighty year old man, his dialysis was becoming harder via veins that frequently collapsed and at some point soon he would bleed, either in the heart or the brain. I sat and listened, feeling sick.

Graham and I had never really talked about much when we were together. We seemed to sit in silence most of the time, but we didn't need words; he would look at me, I would look at him, and that was enough. What could I say that he didn't already know? During one more animated conversation, he told me that after his heart attack, as he was lying on the hospital bed, he had an out-of-body experience. He could see himself lying on the bed. Then he proceeded to describe the emergency room and all the details in it. He told me how I had picked up his jeans and all his change had poured out of a pocket, scattering in all directions. He named everyone who was there and the time on the clock, despite being unconscious the whole time. He looked at me, judging my reaction. I asked, "What did you feel?" He looked at me, and through me, and said, "Nothing, it was like a film and I just thought 'There's me', and no pain. I didn't want to come back, but I knew I had to."

After leaving hospital he moved back to the family home, into a bedroom that had been created for him downstairs. He left hospital on a sunny Monday and was in a very bright mood and glad to be home. He spent the evening talking with Ernie. Mum relates that she had just gone up to bed when she heard Graham screaming for her so she ran down to see what was wrong. He was sobbing, trying to get the words out. He couldn't see, he was panicking and she was trying to comfort him, talk to him, hold him and then he lost consciousness.

I was at home with my boys, just about to go to bed myself at about 11.50 p.m. As I walked up the stairs, I froze. At the top of the stairs I saw a huge mass of sparkles, glittering and suspended in the air. It was beautiful and in the shape of a person, very clearly 'someone' trying to blend together. I was transfixed but not afraid, then started to climb the stairs slowly with a feeling of complete bemusement. At the top, I reached out my hand and felt into the lights as they moved - it tingled and I smiled. It was like diamonds, so beautiful, all gold and light sparkles. In my focused state I heard a voice say very clearly, "Find the music." A song called September Blue came into my head. Oh, I liked that song.

> *You touch the stars at midnight... now I'm standing by your side...*
> *My soul is tired and heavy... I would rather be with you now...*

I didn't want to, but I turned away from the diamonds and said, "I'm going, I'm going", then raced downstairs to find the song on a tape. I found it immediately – strange, as I hadn't known where it was. I knew I had to listen to it. When I reached the stairs again the sparkles had gone and I felt quite disappointed. I couldn't understand why I wasn't scared. There was absolutely no fear, just the most beautiful, tangible feeling; I lay down, hugged the teddy my husband had left me and drifted off.

Twenty minutes later the 'phone rang. It was my mother in a hysterical state, crying that Graham had become unconscious at midnight and had gone to hospital. As I was on my own at home with the boys, I couldn't go to the hospital right away so I made my way there the next morning, after I'd taken the children to school. I was dreading it. Graham had suffered a massive brain haemorrhage. They had done brain stem cell tests and told us that there wasn't much hope.

I had known this was going to happen, but you never believe it until it does and reality hits. I went numb, and immediately morphed myself into coping mode. 'I am strong, I can do this, I have to.' He was in the Intensive Care Unit. I steeled myself and took a deep breath before I entered the bed space. When I saw the breathing apparatus, his chest rising and falling, his pale face and his body just covered with a sheet, I lost it completely and broke down. The strength of my sobs racked my heart; it felt like I had a knife through it and the tears and anguish that followed shocked me to the core. It was a sob the like of which I have never known in all my adult life and I had no control over it. Although I had known that he was close to his time to pass over, the pain was unbearable. Gradually I came back to the moment. Mum had never seen me like that. I had never let anyone see me like that. I pulled myself together and apologised for not being as strong as thought I was.

Graham had three young daughters, such beautiful children, and they loved their Dad. How could this be fair? I sat slumped in a chair by his bed along with Mum, wishing and praying he could recover, and hoping my husband would be back soon. I made a call to his Army unit - they were fantastic and he arrived at 10 p.m. I shall be forever grateful to all who arranged this for me at such a desperate time. About 2.30 a.m. Mum stirred and tried to rise but collapsed at the side of the bed. She'd had no sleep in twenty-four hours and was exhausted. She didn't want to leave her son, but I convinced her to go to the relatives' room to get some sleep while I sat the rest of the night, with my husband dozing nearby, in a chair next to my dying brother.

Graham's heart rate was very high, his will to live very strong even though he was technically brain dead. He'd always said that if ever he was badly injured through racing we were to let him go, but I just thought, "My beautiful brother - don't leave us." When the nurses had changed his sheets they'd pulled his bed away from the wall so you could see all of his head. Graham was bald from the age of twenty and on his scalp now was a massive red blotch; I inhaled sharply and froze, and I knew then it would not be long. I knew what I had to do. I leaned over him, studying his features, stroked him and told him how much he was loved and how special he was. Taking all my courage and keeping my voice level and soft, I whispered, "You need to go now, you can't beat this one. I'll watch over your daughters. It's so much better over there, you know this. You'll be free of all your pain. Go, Graham. We love you. You don't have to do this anymore. Just go… and say 'Hi' to Dad for me." At that moment a tear rolled down his cheek and I knew he could hear me, whether he was sitting on the ceiling as he'd done before or there was some vestige of a miracle there.

After our one-sided chat, his heart rate started to slow down rapidly and his vital functions started to cease. It was as if he had heard me say it was all right, he had permission to go. He had suffered so much in his thirty-eight years, not just with his body but with the divorce and relationship betrayal, and he was very sensitive. It hurt him so much.

Mum could not make the decision to turn off the life support machine, so I did. It was time. Well, I wanted my brother to be better, but that just wasn't going to happen. When the doctors asked us what we wanted to do, Mum was crying so hard my heart ached for her; so I turned to Graham, sent him a silent "So sorry, I love you, I hope I'm doing the right thing as you would wish it", and told them to continue. They flicked the switch - such a simple gesture. When he passed there was a feeling of great peace in the room for all of us, as if the waiting for him to go was the worst thing. I felt no need to stay with his body; I knew he wasn't there anymore and besides I felt him with me. The gang of four was now three.

It was Graham's death that got me through the doors of a Spiritualist church. Mum was advised by a doctor to have counselling to deal with her grief. It consumed her every day and she was an emotional mess, flatly refusing any drugs. I was not much better but at least I knew Graham was fine; I've always had this overriding faith and belief. When she asked me to go with her to the church, I refused at first. I was vehement, stamping around while all the time she was pleading with me. No! No! No! I was suddenly afraid. All the scary experiences I'd had as a child made me think, 'No way! Been there, done that.' But my Mum is very good at emotional blackmail, and she pleaded and begged so much that eventually I couldn't turn her down. She really had no-one else to go with her. Martin would never ever have gone – he'd always called me 'a nut job' - and Andy lived in America by this time. But I told her that if anything spooky started happening, I was out of there. She agreed.

The church was small and we were welcomed the moment we walked in. I felt a bit unsure, out of my depth, and tried scowling to keep everyone away from me. I didn't know what to expect. I'd always been good at hiding behind a tough façade, but really my stomach was in knots. During the service there were prayers and singing, and then the medium started to talk on the philosophy of Spiritualism. He talked about having a connection with spirit, but not understanding the form it takes. I grudgingly had to admit I was fascinated. I hung on his every word as he answered every question that flowed in and out of my mind. Then the messages began, and I watched people's faces as they seemed to know what he was talking about. How could he do that? The service ended and there was no message for us.

We were just about to walk out and I was mumbling to my Mum "I told you there was no point" when the medium came running up and asked to speak to us privately. We stared at each other, and then followed this tall, thin man to the room at the back of the church. We sat down and he went quiet, composing himself, and then he started to talk, describing a man. I knew instantly it was Graham as he was talking about a life support mask. He described Graham with absolute accuracy, what he liked and disliked, his pleasures, his family. We were absolutely astounded. I couldn't believe that this person knew such details when we had never met him before. How could he have a conversation with 'them'? They just scared the heck out of me and made a lot of noise!

It was nothing less than a life-changing experience, a paradigm shift. We drove home in silence, half scared, half exhilarated, because I knew deep within me that I'd found what I was looking for. Was I brave enough? Yes I was. This is when my spiritual life began the second time around… and Graham was the catalyst.

Mum rarely went back to the church after that; she had what she needed at that time. But I started to go to the service every Sunday evening, listening eagerly. I have to say that some of it did not ring true to me, and some I just could not accept. Quite honestly, some of it was the biggest load of rubbish but then some was amazing, life changing and beautiful. Spirit has the capacity to do that, to completely change your life.

I had always been rebellious. I would not take advice or help. No-one could tell me anything that I would listen to. I doubted everything. But I hadn't been going to the church very long when I had an epiphany. Everything that I'd experienced, everything that I'd tried to reason with, everything that I'd heard and seen, suddenly started to make sense to me. I understood that I was part of the spiritual realm because I am spirit too. I came from it, I am it now, and I shall return to that state when I die. It was a very welcome and comforting revelation. I was not different after all, there were others like me - I was like them, this was me, really me. I belonged, I was accepted and I was home. I came to love being in this church, this lovely little haven where I could be me, with this warm close feeling; this is still the case even now.

At this point of my journey, my serious spiritual understanding began, with knowledge of death and life - as much as anyone can know on this Earth. There is so much wisdom to share, through life's experiences. Although I'd thought I had experienced enough, and my heart still ached with losing Graham, it now seemed there was a plan. Maybe he knew that. This was my beginning, and also his.

When you listen to the words from the spirit world, either philosophy or messages, it's very important to make your own mind up. Do you believe it? Does it resonate somewhere? We always have a choice. We do not have to accept everything we are told. We all have a rebellious side, so guide it to surface when you need that strength, at a time of your choosing.

CHAPTER SIX

Another Beginning

I gradually started to understand, it was all real. Everything I had gone through to this point was a fine plan and now it was time to stand up and do something about it. But I was just too scared. How could I get rid of that fear? Maybe they could just take it away for a while? Yes, I shall ask them.

Graham's death had a great effect on me. I didn't discuss it with anyone, mainly because I couldn't. It was just too personal. I seemed fine as always, but something changed when he went. One of my brothers was no longer here. Sometimes you just can't get your head around it when people die so young. It is so hard to grasp the idea that it's their pathway and that they will not be here anymore. When someone very close dies, the people left behind often start to look at life very differently; details that mattered before do not matter anymore and life becomes much simpler in some ways. But as for the pain, it just goes on. I learned very quickly that even though we may have some knowledge of the spirit world we all have to go through the pain of loss and grief. We feel it to the core and it moves us irrevocably forward spiritually, whether we know it or not.

I thought back to how I sat in the sunshine with Graham, not long before he passed. I massaged his feet and he told me how wonderful it made him feel and that I should do more of this, so about six months later I enrolled at a local college to attend a course on reflexology. One problem – I hadn't got the funds required. But if you are meant to do something for spirit, you will. I asked spirit for help and lo and behold the funds became available. I knew it was meant to be. This course took three years to complete; I found it quite easy and received so much joy seeing how people reacted to the treatment. I seemed always to know exactly where to touch. I didn't really know how, and I didn't always look or ask. I just accepted that this was something I could do, which was a first for me – I'd thought I had no talents at all.

I continued to visit the Spiritualist church on a regular basis, attending the services on a Sunday evening, curious as to what it was all about and hoping to learn more about how it all worked. I always had butterflies in my stomach when I went, apprehension mixed with excitement, but I loved it and always felt very comfortable in this environment. The services were lovely, not scary at all and it was all about healing and giving to others. I like that philosophy. There was a short talk - learning about life, different ways to look at situations, seeing the best in people, forcing you to think that maybe there was another view. There was also a session where a medium would give messages to members of the congregation and I loved to watch their faces. When a message hit home, right to the heart of that person, you always saw it in the eyes. Afterwards there were refreshments so people could get together and chat. It was just welcoming and comfortable and the answers to the questions that I'd been wondering about for all those years came thick and fast, as if I were playing catch up. Anything I wanted to know, I would ask and the answer would come. It was hard to hold on for the ride sometimes; every day something new occurred to enlighten me. Within a year I had become a member and was voted onto the committee. Maybe it was not such a passing phase, then?

Around this time I was invited to a friend's development circle. This is group of like-minded people who join together for their spiritual growth and for the good of the spirit world. There are many of these circles all over the county and amazing phenomena can occur. It was light-hearted and I found a sort of acceptance of my spiritual experience as a child within the circle and with these lovely people who were all very different. We were all searching together and that made the journey a little easier. My childhood fear was still ever present, maybe lessening a little over time, but I couldn't shake it off completely. I had to find a way to deal with it so I could continue without too much hindrance, so I found a box inside myself to hide it away. The problem with this is that the box has to be opened eventually…

Developing your spiritual experience in circles is always a gradual progress, or at least it should be; you can't cut corners or hurry it in any way, else they will return you to phase one. There's no fast track to working for the spirit world. Everyone has to work hard, put in the time and live in the here and now. The spirit energies are natural, strong and beautiful and always there when you need them, whenever you need them. The growth is always subtle. You are being desensitised gradually over time. It's a bit like snakes and ladders, so keep away from the snakes. You will always be led to the circle or group you should be attending, so just ask and it will appear in your life - as everything you need always does.

I was quite happy just to attend small circles here and there. I remember saying to people that there was no way that I could stand up and do this medium stuff, it just filled me with dread. It really took me a long time to work for the spirit world. I never thought I would be good enough. After all, I was just little insignificant me who was scared of people, places and life. I was a nobody. Why would I even begin to believe I could do this? I could not get over my personal lack of worthiness.

The spirit world can often be very noisy at night. I had not been disturbed too much since the childhood episodes; I asked them to leave me alone overnight and they usually complied. Then one particular night I was curled up in bed slumbering peacefully, when I was pulled back into consciousness by the loudest noise. It sounded close. With heart racing and feeling a throbbing pulse in my throat and ears, I listened: 'Boom!' I was petrified. It sounded like a gunshot! I immediately woke my husband and told him, panic-stricken, that I thought there was someone in the house with a gun. He went downstairs and searched the entire house inside and out, but found nothing to cause the noise. The children hadn't awoken and neither had he. He held me, calming me as he told me I must have been dreaming. But I knew it wasn't a dream. Over time I discussed this event with many people and discovered it was the sound of dimensions clashing, all to do with 'energy'. Ah yes, energy!

A year or so after I started going to the church, a regular Wednesday night get-together at my home began, which came to be known as The Curry Club. It started with a few friends from work and friends of friends. Initially there were about eight of us crammed around my dining table or on the floor of the lounge. We would eat curry, chat, laugh and put the world to rights; we told jokes, discussed problems and talked about 'strange spooky happenings' - our favourite subject by far. It was a friendly, safe environment where we could discuss our lives and progress in the here and now. There were some very detailed and heated discussions and it was fascinating that everyone was so open to the possibility of something more than this life. There were many opinions, but it was never about who was right and who was wrong. We had much fun and laughter, and no subject was taboo. We learned from each other.

It was within this group of trusted friends that I started to pass on small bits of information, from whom or where I knew not (and did I really want to know?). I was relaxed, the atmosphere was comfortable, there was no pressure and the words just flowed. Even back then I saw shocked faces as I knew details not previously shared. I understood the information was not from me, but through me; I heard it in my mind and just said it as it was relayed to me. Yes, I did ask who it was, but there was silence in return.

I found I could bring much comfort, love and assistance to the people who came as they all needed words of reassurance. I wanted to help and I could, it was simple. This was my time to grow and to blossom. It was all much easier to accept because I was relaxed and comfortable in easy surroundings, and I was lucky to have the opportunity and the people to do it with. All who attended then are still in touch with each other and the spirituality we learned and observed has assisted us all. Importantly, those evenings taught me the basics of how to speak to people in a way that they can accept what I'm saying, always being respectful to them. It is a great responsibility to bring forward the correct information, with the same reverence and respect you would show to your own loved ones. But it is also crucial to respect the connection you have with the spirit world and to work hard to hone that spiritual connection, to give the most accurate information you can. Within this safe environment I could push the barriers and still get the message across, and it was truly humbling. Week after week for a few years, people arrived on a Wednesday for whatever they needed - and the curry of course, it was good curry too. Gradually I started to understand why people came and what they each needed; it was a great experience and one I know we will all treasure.

Whenever I meet anyone now with the intention of reading for them, I know what they want, what they yearn for and what they need - as does spirit. It's a call on a deeper level, from soul to soul. I am so grateful to every one of those beautiful people who turned up week after week to create the atmosphere of love and understanding and, yes, sometimes confusion; but eventually understanding would come and the purpose of it solidified into all our lives. This became a development circle. One man did tell me that he heard nothing and his guides were a bunch of beer-swilling amateurs! But nevertheless he is the kindest and best of men, assisting everyone he meets, so he is working for spirit in his own special way.

It is said that when the pupil is ready the teacher appears, and that is what happened to me. Spirit had its work cut out - I was never going to come quietly, always wanting answers first, doubting everything. My teacher's name was Lilian (and she will always be my teacher). She asked me if I would like to attend a circle she was putting together. This came out of the blue. I had been asking for help at that time, eager to move onto the next part but didn't have a clue what to do or how to do it. So spirit sent me an angel. I arrived for the group on a Monday evening; there were seven of us in total, I knew only one other person and was very self-conscious. I turned up with a book and Lilian took it from me, telling me I didn't need it; I wasn't happy about that, but she was right, she was always right. All you need is within you.

Over time Lilian led us, cajoled us, and encouraged us. She was tough and unrelenting, and it was harder than I ever thought it would be. I had to learn complete discipline, to trust in her and the spirit world – trusting in myself was a little harder. I have to admit I was particularly hard work for her because I was so full of doubt. She would talk to me raising her eyebrows in despair, sometimes with irritation in her voice, but she knew she had to be tough with me; it was what I needed and understood. She encouraged us to find the way we wished to work, to find the energies that were around to assist us and the gifts contained within them. All the time she stressed the necessity for correct teaching, for having respect for all in the spirit world and in this world, and for the correct intention in wanting to develop the communication skills.

To this day intention is everything to me, and it's the first question I ask anyone who wants to work for spirit and to look within themselves. What do you want to do and why? Are you prepared for the ride? It can get very bumpy. I agonised over these questions for years, not sure if I actually wanted to do anything; why I would want to expose myself again to ridicule? But it's simple really. "If you're meant to work for the spirit world, you will," Lilian told me. I scoffed at that; I was interested in searching to make sense of the past, but working for spirit was not something I had ever planned. Week after week we were led in different exercises, and I was shocked every time that something I did worked. But really it's not so complicated; we just have to feel the energy with our hearts.

At that time I was quietly content attending circles, I didn't want to go any further into churches and do services or demonstrations. That prospect was very scary and I recoiled in horror whenever it was mentioned. I just couldn't let go of that fear, couldn't imagine being the centre of attention. No, I was content to sit in the shadows. But the next step was decided for me, as so many have been since; not quite what I had in mind though.

We had a beginners' circle at the church each week on a Friday. One particular night I received a telephone call asking if I would stand in for the circle leader as no-one else could do it and we couldn't let people down as some travelled quite a way to get there. So, very flippantly, I said I would do it. As soon as I put the `phone down, I felt horrified. Why did I say that? What I was going to do? I thought, 'I'm no teacher, I can't do this. Oh my God, help me.' That first evening I just went with it, followed my instinct and not even thinking about it; there was no stuttering, as if it never existed. I was talking, discussing, advising, but it didn't feel like me doing this. I was told that some of the wisdom was beautiful, but I couldn't remember much of what I'd said. It became pretty clear over time that someone else in spirit was in charge, and I need not remember the details because they're not for me.

My confidence grew week on week. More people attended and I started to wonder where this was going. When I talked, I seemed to know details I didn't know I knew. It was all very confusing, but then I was growing too alongside everyone else. We are always learning, every day. I started to trust. I learned that any development circle is led by the spirit world; they are always present and in charge. The circle leader is just someone who is watching over the physical presence of those attending. They may hear, see or sense spirit a little more, but no-one is any better than the next person; it's just that some are a little further along their path than others.

Teaching other people is a great responsibility. One must work with the highest ideals, morals, intention and dedication, and there can be no compromise.

The circle became very popular and one night I had forty-six people attending. I was very tired after that night! I always made it fun and interesting, always gave them somewhere to go in visualisation, and it seemed to go well no matter who was there. Those who were meant to be there would be there, and it was not for me to judge the needs or level of anyone else. Each is moving along at their own correct pace which, incidentally, will never be the same as someone else's. Sometimes we just have to trust, and allow everyone to find their truth and their path. It takes time, love, honesty and strength.

To give with compassion to people in their hour of need is very humbling and a necessary part of life. To pass on a message from a loved one in the spirit world to someone close to them here is the best experience in the world for me. To see someone cry bitter-sweet tears for their lost loved ones, and the fact that they have chosen to come to me to give them that experience, moves me so much. I will always remember the day I finally relented; I just threw the towel in and stopped fighting myself. Knowing so much had happened in my life, how much worse could it be?

From day one when I agreed to work for spirit, I said that they must bring to me those whom they wished me to speak to. Nowadays I like working in small places as well as at big events because I believe that everyone has the right and should have the opportunity to contact their loved ones in spirit. There are many who can't afford expensive events but they may have a pound to put in the collection box on a Sunday night, and they are just as important as everyone else. And I always believe that no matter where I go the people there are meant to be there, whether there are three or thirty or three hundred. Spirit always brings me the people I need to see; that is part of my contract with them. This love connection is so needed. I hear people talk about books they've read about those who have passed over, about how they are never alone, and they are happy to know that about the spirit world. But people also need to know that they are not alone here and now, and that the capacity for more in their lives is so great.

To anyone interested in having a reading with a medium, I urge you to choose yours carefully. I have found that there are some unsavoury people out there who will not be honest with you and will give the rest of us true workers a bad name. Trust your instincts. Only you will know if they are right for you. Ask for details about the medium and don't just go without checking them out; many people just trust blindly and end up becoming very distressed. Many times I have had to repair the pain of a person who has been to an unscrupulous medium, and restore their equilibrium when their lives have been shaken to the core. It makes me very angry.

Many times I have known people rush in headlong wanting to be a medium; I can't understand for the life of me why anyone would want to do this job, but they do. I didn't have a choice. Well, I suppose I could have walked away and hid in some dark corner of my life, but the promise of so much more just screamed at me and when I reached that point they knew I couldn't walk away. They knew this was always what I was supposed to do; it was a calling. It was just that I had to under-stand and recognise this, and they never gave up on me. So if you believe it to be your path, don't give up; keep going, have faith and let spirit lead you, and all will be well. They will allow you to go off on your own way and do your own thing, because you have complete personal responsibility in your life. Oh yes, you make your own choices, so you cannot blame anyone else. But then they always help to bring you back onto the path you have diverted from. We all do that. Sometimes we go backwards, or it seems like that, but you can learn to listen to that inner voice we all have; it is ever present and it urges us onwards.

If you do wish to work with the spirit energies you must start to un-derstand what is involved in this work and how it can affect your life and your physical body. It is very important to live in the now, in the mo-ment, and not get carried away. You have to be grounded. You must try not to be judgemental, either to yourselves or to others. Now I can hear you saying, "I don't do that." Oh yes, you do. We all do, whether we realise it or not. We always have a judgement about every person and situation we meet in this life and it's a very difficult habit to break. It starts as just a thought in our minds, then grows and can get out of hand pretty quickly. Please understand that a thought is a real entity in its own right, and all thoughts are heard and held in 'the spiritual Internet'.

No-one judges us in the spirit world no matter what thoughts we have or what we do; only we will do that, only we will know the effects of this life experience. We will realise that when we arrive in the level of the spirit world where we belong. Being aware of this has made me practise non-judgement in my life much more. Even those whom I know have hurt me, been rude to me and stuck a knife in my back, so to speak - I do not judge them, how could I? We are all imperfect, or we would not be here at all, for everyone has a purpose to fulfil.

Working for spirit causes changes in us. We have to make changes in our lives in so many ways, and it's not easy. We have to examine our lives more closely than we have ever done, find out what is not working and do what is necessary to change it. Sounds easy? I assure you it isn't. I find it difficult to convey in words the complexity and beauty of the effect of spirit in our lives. We have to experience it to understand it, and we don't have to want to work for spirit to do this.

Sometimes you may want to work for spirit in one particular way and that is all you want to do. Good luck with that, but you will only do it if you are meant to; remember, there is always a plan and we are not aware of it in the everyday physical world. Imagine you are in a department store, a store of spiritual gifts. You want one particular gift, for example to be a medium, so you get in the lift and press the button for that particular floor. But the lift doesn't stop on that floor, it takes you to another one, say, the healing floor, but you didn't want to do healing. So what do you do? Now you have a choice. You will have the gift that you have, what you are meant to do. There are many ways to work for spirit. Some people may never have any mediumistic tendencies but they sit in development circles for many years with that intention and just have silence, feeling nothing. If this is you, and you are not happy, then take the hint. On the other hand, some may be 'energy pods', providing the energy for the circle because spirit have some special purpose in mind. Some may work for spirit on the Earth listening, counselling, caring, helping and giving of their time for others. Some are working for this beautiful Earth herself, keeping her balanced so we can live here. Indeed, some people are just powerhouses of energy who help others.

We should all learn to give a little more to one another, and understand each other as human to human (which is the same as spirit to spirit). We should give a little more, feel a little more and love a little more. If we all did that every day, we could achieve so much in this world. I have always wanted to love and to heal the whole world, and I'm told all the time "You can't do that", but it's not going to stop me trying. I send thoughts of love and healing for many each day, hoping their lives will be eased and the pain healed. I send thoughts for this beautiful Mother Earth that we live on and abuse, and pray that she sustains us. For any I hear of who pass over or are ill, I send love to their families whether I know them or not.

After all I've been through myself, I know how it feels. How I wish I'd had someone to pray for me when I needed it, whether I'd believed it worked or not.

CHAPTER SEVEN

The End of an Era

I thought, "But why me? Why am I the one to have to sit and be his wing man now?" It was a sudden realisation. I knew I had to forgive him for all the anger, all the things he did to me, the anguish he caused me. Could I do this?

Ernie fell ill in November, 2005. It was my birthday. He was at home and by this time quite unsteady on his feet. That morning he had reached to pick up a newspaper from the front doormat, stumbled and fell and couldn't get back up again. Mum tried her best to raise him to his feet but she couldn't manage it. She rang for an ambulance, but they couldn't get him to stand either so they took him into hospital. He was confused and upset. I got the call and went to Mum; she always relied on me to be there.

We went in to see him that afternoon, changed him and made him comfortable, and I noticed for the first time just how much weight he'd lost. His bones were sticking through his skin and he was effectively just a shadow of his former self. He could not sit up to eat, just didn't have the strength. I sat at his back to push him up and the nurses told me off, and told him not expect such help from them. Indeed, his treatment in the hospital was sadly lacking and instead of treating him and getting him up and about with some physiotherapy, they just left him lying in bed, a sad eighty-two year old. He needed twenty-four hour nursing care. Mum tried desperately to get him moved to another hospital, one that he had been treated in before, and eventually he was transferred.

It had been some days since I'd seen him last. I walked into his ward and studied him lying there, so frail and old, so in need of compassion. I was not prepared for the emotion that hit me at that moment. Was I to show him compassion when he had been so unkind to me? Was I to lead by example? I knew that he was not long for this world. I just didn't know if I could be the one to sit there and watch him go through all that. Why would I? I remember being quite angry. I didn't want to do this at all. It's really unfair to have to lose two Dads, I thought. A strange thought, considering. Mum, bless her, didn't realise how ill he was. She would not or could not grasp it.

I stomped petulantly out of the ward feeling both quite mad and sad for him. I walked up and down grumbling to spirit, "It's not fair. Why do I have to be with him when he dies? Can't someone else do it? I can't do it. It's so unfair." I could feel them around me - the love, the arms - so I closed my eyes and stilled and leaned against the wall with my head bowed. I flinched as I felt an invisible hand on my shoulder, then a voice said quietly and meaningfully, "But you have to, you know you do." Yes, it was part of what needed to be done, part of my journey, part of my learning and progression. I was crying and angry, so I ran and went home to hide.

The next day was Christmas Eve and my husband and I were getting ready to go into town to buy last minute food we needed for Christmas lunch. Mum called saying the hospital had 'phoned and someone needed to go in and speak to the doctors. She said she was too busy to go, but I knew she just couldn't handle sitting beside his hospital bed watching him die. I swallowed very hard, feeling like I had a lump of metal in my chest, and said I would go. I knew I had to.

My husband gave me a lift to the hospital. Deep in thought and trepidation I slowly ambled to the ward, not wanting to hurry, found a chair and sat by him. I stared for ages trying to acclimatise to the situation unfolding before me. He was not responsive, just sleeping, and I sat very still thinking of all the things he had done to me and how much I had disliked him over the years. I thought how sad I felt for him now, how life changes our roles.

Now I was the powerful one and I could walk away at any moment and leave him; it was my choice. But I knew I wouldn't do that.

I was still trying to think how I was going to cope with this when I was aware that a doctor had his hand on my shoulder and was asking to speak to me in private. We went to an empty room, cold and clinical; I sat down and felt quite sick. The doctor quietly explained me to me that nothing else could be done to help him because his body was beginning to shut down. I'd known he was poorly, but to hear that said makes it real. He said he would answer any questions I had, but I had to get out of there. Mumbling something, I hurriedly went outside and, trying to hold it together, called my Mum.

I wandered back and sat by his bed studying his hands. He had such long fingers. He was still wearing his wedding ring, now very loose. As I stroked his arm, his skin almost seemed to break away. I held his hand - something I had never done before. Mine was very small compared to his. I sat there watching, transfixed, a lump in my throat as big as an orange, with such conflicting emotions. 'No! I am not going to cry.' I was strong for everyone, that's me, and I had never lost it - at least not since Graham passed. 'How strong am I?' I had to be. I knew I would be needed, to help Mum.

When it came I had no warning, like a wave cleansing all before it. I can't even say what sparked it, but huge therapeutic sobs just took over me. I was feeling so many mixed emotions – anger, sadness, pain, forgiveness – that my head throbbed like it was going to explode. So much history between us and most of it painful, but did it matter now? He had always been such a big, imposing, authoritative and healthy man and now his body was just giving up. I thought, 'But why me? Why am I the one to have to sit and be his wing man now?' It was a sudden realisation. I knew I had to forgive him for all the anger, all the things he did to me, the anguish he caused me. Could I do this? Forgive him for everything?

Yes, I could. I realised I had to tell him this - he had to know it before he passed. 'Difficult' does not cover how it felt talking to him, even though he was unconscious. But I couldn't let him go to spirit without knowing that. I knew he would need that gift when he faced himself in the spirit world and saw the truth of all his actions.

Periodically Ernie would open his eyes and look at me. He couldn't speak but there was recognition in his eyes and he stared at me. He looked so tired, and a little scared. I held his hand and just tried to be my normal breezy self, chatting to him and talking about anything that came into my head. He would drift in and out of sleep, and that's when I recalled the painful memories, so many of them. He woke up early in the afternoon, stared around and seemed to know where he was for the first time. He lowered his eyes to mine. I smiled and just stared at him. He stared back and I could see a resignation to fate in his eyes. I whispered, "It's time to rest now, it's ok, you're not alone." He stared at me with sad, frightened eyes, then nodded slightly and went back to sleep. He had such a terrible fear of dying that, no matter what my feelings were, I couldn't have left him on his own then. Mum arrived not long after and we both sat talking into the evening by his bed, holding his hand and reminiscing. She lives very much in this world and she made me laugh; I was grateful for that.

By six o'clock I was exhausted, mentally and physically drained. I thought I had done enough. I rested my head against his bed and said, "I want to go home now." Then a voice quite audibly and clearly said, "You can leave at eight o'clock, not before." I looked around to see if anyone else was registering the voice, but as usual it was only me. Mum asked, "Shall we go? You look exhausted." I told her that we would leave at eight o'clock. She asked me why and I said, "I have absolutely no idea" and told her what I'd heard. She shrugged and said, quite matter-of-factly, "Oh, ok." I smiled, she believed me now.

From that point onwards he rarely opened his eyes. I was suddenly brought back from my silent reveries, aware of someone from spirit standing next to him. It was a lady, and I knew she was here for him. It was comforting, knowing that spirit was close, waiting to help him cross over. Just before eight o'clock I heard noises on the outside of the curtain, shuffling noises and whispering. I peered over at Mum, questioningly. She just pulled that 'I haven't a clue' face. Then the music started. A local silver band had come into the ward to play hymns and they had surrounded us. Tears welled in my eyes; it was such a poignant moment - one I shall never forget. A man so close to death, and yet such beautiful music at a time when it was needed. It was like they were playing him onward and upward. Well, after all, it was Christmas Eve.

In that moment, I felt the spirits' presence and the most wonderful feeling of strength, a powerful and loving hug, not of this world. I looked down at Ernie and he opened his eyes, listening to them play, and then closed them again just as quickly with a flicker of a smile on his lips. There was such a feeling of peace and love around him. I could not begrudge him that. The band stopped playing at exactly eight o'clock. He shifted slightly and drifted back off to sleep. We left the hospital soon afterwards. I knew that I had witnessed something quite beautiful. And that I would not see him alive again.

Strolling back to the car I felt bruised, empty and sore. I was so exhausted. The only thing I wanted to do was have a nice hot bath and drift in the water away from this world to where I meet with my beautiful friends in spirit - to ease my pain, to fix me. When I reached home I found that my wonderful husband had done all the preparations for the Christmas Day lunch. I was grateful as I knew we would have to go ahead as normally as possible. He decided to pop down to the local pub for a pint, so I took advantage of having the house to myself and ran a steaming hot bath.

As I was lying there with my eyes closed, the water was soothing, cleansing. I thought about Ernie, how I'd perceived him, and I knew I had to let go of what I was carrying and hoped he would know that I forgave him. Today had been harder than I ever knew it could be. Trying to forget everything, I sank down lower into the warm water and as I lay there I started to drift. The house was totally dark and silent, only the bathroom light was on. I was trying to visualise somewhere lovely in my mind where I could escape.

But suddenly my senses were dragged back to the here and now by a loud beeping noise. It didn't stop but got even louder, so I climbed out of the bath to investigate. Still dripping I stepped out onto the landing to listen for the noise, which seemed to be coming from my youngest son's bedroom. Now, each year Thomas would go and stay with his father over Christmas. He had not been in the house for over a week, and no-one had been in his bedroom. I opened the door and entered, not thinking to turn on the light, and next to the bed I could see a light blinking. Thomas had an alarm clock that he never used and it had sat there unused for years. It was in the shape of a football which needed manual switching to turn on and off. Now it was belting out its alarm and the illuminated hands indicated the time was 6.50 p.m. I then heard a tap on the door, but I was too tired and too emotional to play. I put the clock down and walked out of the room, smiling to myself, taking no notice of the knocks. "Sorry, I have to ignore you for the moment, I just can't listen." But it was comforting to know they were there.

At 6.50 a.m. on Christmas Day, I got a `phone call from my Mum saying that Ernie had passed away in his sleep. Christmas was a bit of a blur that year and the days that followed were filled with making the necessary funeral arrangements. Mum was absolutely devastated of course. They had been married for over thirty years.

Life went on as it always does. About six months later, I decided on the spur of the moment to go and complete some paperwork at the Spiritualist church, where I'd been Committee Secretary for years. It was a Wednesday afternoon and there was a service just commencing; I went to work in the office at the back of the church. After the service the medium who had been working during the service came to find me and said there was a message for me. We sat in the office and she told me there was a man called Ernie there who wanted to talk to me. I was somewhat surprised - I hadn't expected to hear from him, I thought we were done. The medium said that Ernie wanted to apologise for what he had done to me and how he had treated me.

I was amazed because I had never expected to hear that. It was all I had wanted to hear when he was alive, but now I had already forgiven him. I realised he was only able to hurt me because I let him. He took all his anger and unhappiness out on me, and I gave my power to him - although I didn't realise that at the time. We all are so much more powerful than we give ourselves credit for, and we always hurt the ones we care about. Why? Because we can. But we still have a huge capacity to forgive, and we should at least try. Why? Because we can. Hanging on to all our negativity brings us nothing but trouble; it clouds our path and stops us making the right decisions. We must let it go, stop blaming ourselves, resolve those feelings and move on with a clearer heart.

Ernie is still missed, but at last I can talk about him now with a softer edge of forgiveness.

People in the spirit world find it favourable to receive the forgiveness of those they have wronged on this side of life, to be able to move on in their learning. This is not always possible, even though the cause of the problem may be past. To let go of that on this side of life is another problem entirely. At least they know what they have done and can face that at the level they need to, to overcome it and move onward. I had held negative and angry feelings about Ernie for so very long that it was a release finally to forgive him. I felt lighter. I had to let go of the physical feelings of anger and resentment, so that I was able to progress too. We are all linked - no person or situation is by chance, and we are with the people whom we need to be with here and now. They are gifts. Even though we don't always like them, want them or understand them, there is always a reason, always a plan. After all, we have chosen it all before we came here.

Would I have changed anything? Acted differently? No, I don't think so. Would he? I'm sure he wouldn't. Sometimes people arrive in our lives to shake us up, to make us angry and question things, to make us think in ways we would never have done if we had not endured that experience. And we all need the balance of good and bad, to realise the difference. I pray that we all find the strength to let go of our Earthly pains, stresses and situations and find some peace.

CHAPTER EIGHT

Martín

*He was handsome, smart and very charming, and the ladies
loved him. He always knew he had a magical charm that could
disarm people in seconds (and he used it to his advantage).
He knew how to make people laugh and how the
laughter affected everyone.*

Whenever I think of my brother Martin I feel a little angry. Angry
because he never made the changes needed for his life to be happy and
contented. Angry because underneath he was such a lovely person to so
many people, but suffered inner turmoil and pain. And angry because
he never gave the kindness and value to himself half as much as he did
to others. He was also angry, but funny and caring too; I just wish he
could have been happy for once in his life.

Martin was the second son. He was the bad boy, the black sheep.
He had big brown eyes and was always very handsome. When we were
young, Martin was the one who always fought with us all; it was just his
way, he was a very physical person and quick tempered. Once, Martin
and Andy had a big fight in the street over a petty disagreement. Both
of them got bloody noses and Martin ended up in hospital. Our poor
Mum was very stressed on many occasions by the mischief he got up to.
Martin was a myriad of opposites and clashes throughout his life and he
seemed to fall from one mess to another; but it was never his fault, of
course – he always blamed someone else.

One day Martin and I were arguing as usual - we were only teenagers and we always argued. He hit me first and gave me a bleeding nose, but I gave him as good as I got; that comes with the territory, being brought up with boys - you learn to roll with the punches. The boys treated me the same as each other and the fact that I was a girl was never in the equation. Mind you, as I got older they did teach me how to defend myself and, most importantly, we grew up understanding sibling love. However, Graham once literally attempted to strangle Martin – one morning they had got up for work and Graham was angry with Martin for going into his room and taking something that belonged to him without asking. When they were both downstairs, Graham flew across the room and grabbed him by the throat, dragging him to the floor then picking up a brass candlestick to whack him. Mum managed to grab it off him in time and call Ernie to come and intervene.

It seemed like Martin was always in trouble with everyone. Three of us went to the same school and I was two years below him. It was a very large modern comprehensive on two sites. He frequented a group of boys that were considered the tough nuts - big, ugly and mean. He came across as tough and he was; but I just saw him as my brother and, to his credit, he was always very protective of me. On one occasion when I was having trouble with a boy who was teasing me about my stuttering, Martin found out and had a chat - the boy went flying over two desks! After that I was left alone and grateful.

He was always trying to be bigger and bolder than everyone else, loud and funny but with such infectious charm you just couldn't resist him. When I was about eighteen I arrived home from work and he was complaining because he didn't have any money; he gave me a sob story about how he'd promised to go out that night and meet someone but he had no money to do so. He utterly charmed me with his big brown eyes so I gave him ten pounds (and I only earned twenty-eight pounds a week). He smiled and said, "Thanks, sis." He went out to party with the ladies, typically, and I never did get it back.

When Martin left school, he became a vehicle technician. He loved fixing things and he was very talented. He progressed up the career ladder, moving to Coventry and then to Nuneaton. At his first job he met Bob, who became his best friend throughout life. Bob had a boat down on the south coast and they would go away for weekends. Martin loved it. They were some of his happiest times.

In his early twenties he was very well known in the town. He was handsome, smart and very charming, and the ladies loved him. He always knew he had a magical charm that could disarm people in seconds (and he used it to his advantage). He would make us laugh by breaking into impressions and falling about like an oaf. He knew how to make people laugh and how the laughter affected everyone. People would have given him anything - he definitely knew how to get his own way.

As Martin moved into his late twenties he met a lady and got married, but it was a tempestuous and fractious relationship, and it was no surprise that it didn't last. He stumbled along through his life until in 1997 things got much worse. At that time he was living with a partner who had four children. Martin had been around while the children were growing up and he considered them to be his own. Suddenly, one of the girls died aged just seventeen of a heart and lung problem, rare and undetected. He was absolutely inconsolable. A few days later I was woken by the telephone ringing at about 1.30 a.m. I answered it and heard sobbing on the other end. I was awake within seconds and sat on the edge of the bed; I knew my brothers very well and knew it was Martin. He was mumbling incoherently, obviously very drunk. He said it wasn't fair that his daughter had died and he couldn't cope with the loss of her, and why would God want to take such a beautiful creature, and he wanted to kill himself.

Grief was not something that Martin could handle or understand - indeed, years before when our Dad died, he had never cried. So to hear him like this was serious. He told me that life wasn't worth living. Although I tried to explain to him that it's nothing to do with God whatsoever when we die or how we die, he wouldn't listen. He wouldn't have it any other way, he just didn't believe in anything at all. I spent hours on the `phone, soothing him, calming him and trying to make him understand that he could not, and should not, take his own life. I begged him to tell me where he was, but he wouldn't. I asked him to come and see me, but he wouldn't. When the call ended the dawn was rising. We had talked all night. We had never done that, in fact I don't think he'd ever talked to anyone like that. The next day I called him and was very relieved that he was still there.

The relationship between Martin and his elder brother Graham was complex. They fought each other, but loved each other equally and became true friends. But Graham died soon after Martin's daughter, and I don't think Martin ever recovered from that time in his life. He left the relationship that he was in and fell into another, which also fell apart before long. He genuinely always seemed to be the victim. Then in 2002 he had his first heart attack. We were all stunned – he was only forty-one years old. Illness then followed him for the rest of his life.

In 2007 Martin again asked to borrow money from the family, which unfortunately we did not have to give him. He rang me sounding really desperate and I felt bad for him, so I asked our brother Andy who was living in America. We all knew that Martin had borrowed money before from the family and never repaid it, but he told us that he was going to be evicted and he needed the money for rent as he'd lost his job. Andy listened patiently to me; I knew that he didn't want to do it, but he said he would do it for me. He sent the money and we didn't hear from Martin again until a month later, when I asked him if he had the money to repay Andy. He said he would have it in another month, and not to worry because he wouldn't let me down. And then he vanished off the face of the Earth.

We searched for him and discovered that he'd moved out of his flat and no-one knew where he was – there was nothing we could do but wait and see if he surfaced again. In more than a year we didn't hear a word from him. Then Mum received a Mother's Day card from 'Jennifer and Martin'. She didn't have a clue who Jennifer was, but there was a `phone number on the card, so Mum spoke to her and found out that they were engaged. Jennifer had been trying to convince Martin to get back in contact, and Martin didn't know about the sending of the card. She agreed to keep us informed of what Martin was up to and when he was in hospital due to his heart problem. On Christmas Day, Mum plucked up the courage and called Martin to say hello, but he put the `phone down and refused to speak to her. She broke her heart with tears.

Next summer I had a `phone call from him with the usual "Hello, sis." He sounded normal as if we'd only spoken yesterday. He said he needed a favour… He'd just been made redundant again and needed a CV because he wanted to apply for other jobs. I told him to come over to my house, and when I got home he was waiting for me on the driveway. He smiled that boyish smile and my heart sank - he looked ill and drawn. There was no explanation, no apology; he just smiled, disarming me. I did the CV for him and did a check on the local job sites; after a quick search, the first job that came up was to work on military vehicles. He was very interested so I applied for the job for him, there and then. The next morning they called him and said not to worry about an interview, he could start tomorrow. He said later it was the best job he'd ever had. Funny how that happens - you follow a turn of events that leads you just where you need to be. It seemed that he had finally found happiness now.

But only a month later I called in to see Mum, and was amazed to find Martin there, working on the car. When he'd finished we went out into the garden for a chat and a cigarette; he told me that he wasn't feeling well and knew that he was not long for this world. He said he just knew. "Don't worry about it, sis," he said, then he hugged me and said, "I love you, sis." Now I knew this was serious, because Martin had never once told me that he loved me. It was a very special moment for us; we just hugged and stood very still. I quietly asked the spirit world for guidance and there was silence in return. It was an ominous and unnerving feeling. We stayed chatting for a few minutes after that and then he left. Little did I know that this was the last time I would see him alive.

One September evening, I'd been asked to do a reading for a friend's grandmother and left the house just after 7.30 p.m. Whilst driving to my friend's house, a beautiful Michael Jackson track You Are Not Alone was playing, when quite suddenly the atmosphere in the car changed. I can only describe it as the most beautiful spiritual love washing over me so tangibly that it brought tears to my eyes. I turned, almost expecting to see someone sitting in the passenger seat, and said a silent 'thank you' to whoever had been so close to me. I thought to myself that it would be a really good reading with this strength of spirit around.

I was quite buoyant when I arrived at my friend's house, but at that moment my mobile rang. It was my Mum. She was hysterical – crying, shouting "Martin's gone! Martin's gone!" I couldn't grasp what she was saying and asked, "Where has he gone?" She replied "He's dead." The shock that coursed through me at that point, I could never describe. There are just no words. The pain in my heart was all-consuming and I dropped to my knees and screamed. My friend came running down the stairs and all I could say was that my brother was dead and I had to go. I got in the car and drove home. I was so angry; I screamed and shouted all the way. How could he die like this? My husband drove me to collect Mum and my son, and we went to Martin's flat.

It was a heart attack. He had come home from work, had a beer, walked back from the kitchen and sat down at the table, then slumped down to the floor. All the arteries of his heart had closed at the same time. The paramedics had desperately tried to revive him, but by the time we arrived he'd been moved to the bedroom and placed under the quilt as if he were sleeping. Mum wanted to see him, to say goodbye to another son. She was sobbing, talking to him, stroking him, one of the most heart-wrenching scenes I have ever witnessed.

Suddenly I was very aware that he was standing beside me and that he was confused. Now, when I link to the spirit world it almost feels as natural as this one; I just do it with no effort involved. I closed my eyes and tried to explain to him what had happened, and I told him to leave because he didn't need to be here anymore. I kept this to myself and it distressed me immensely. On the way home I prayed hard to my friends and Graham to help him pass over. Friday was an autopilot day, arranging the funeral; sore and bruised, it passed quickly. The next day reality set in and a bucket of tears flowed. I felt empty. How Mum felt, I can't imagine. How do you even begin to cope with losing two husbands and two sons?

I was alone at home. It was a lovely fresh morning with the sun shining through the trees in the garden. I have a lot of trees in my garden, and I love them; they heal me. So I took a cup of coffee and sat in a corner, feeling the peace of nature. I was bereft, I wanted my brother back. Tears would come and then stop.

I closed my eyes and focussed and was suddenly aware of my very lovely spirit friend. I knew spirit had been with me all along. I could feel them, but they had kept quiet as they usually do when I am wrapped in my grief. They let me be for a while, but I was angry. I said, "I know you're there and I don't want to talk to you, so go away" and I heard a voice as crystal clear as any on this Earth say, "Go to the churchyard." I said, "I don't go to churchyards, you know that. I'm not going." The voice kept saying it, quietly but firmly over and over again, with no explanation, just insisting. After a few minutes of this, I stamped petulantly inside, grabbed my keys muttering to myself and drove to the churchyard. The Garden of Remembrance there is very pretty with a seat under a beautiful tree that looks across the manicured church-yard to the war memorial, and beyond that to the pub where we had all spent so many fun nights in times past. Graham's ashes were interred here as well; it's a truly beautiful, tranquil place. But I just did not do churchyards, not since I was a child. It's not as if anyone is there; it's for the living and I knew better. Dragging my feet, I walked up the path to the seat in the Garden of Remembrance, sat down and closed my eyes. I felt the sun on my face and body, warm and comforting. I felt nothing else, I became an empty shell.

Literally a second later, I found myself looking around a long garden. To say that I was surprised is an understatement. I thought 'Am I actually here?' The garden was surrounded by a high, thick, grey stone wall. It had a deep border about eight feet wide with every flower of every colour you could imagine. It was breathtaking. There was a stone circle in the middle of the grassy area and there were two deckchairs, the kind you would find at any beach, brightly striped. Not too sure what I should do, nor what I was doing there, I sat down on one of the chairs and looked around me. As I turned my face to the front, there was an American Indian man there, someone who is very familiar to me and has been with me spiritually for a long time. His eyes were deep and com-passionate and he looked intently at me, full of love and care. I knew he was waiting for me to speak. There were many things I could have said, but I knew time was short so I had to make it count. I didn't feel at all scared, just a little angry and frustrated, but that wasn't his fault.

I asked him if Martin was all right and he said, quietly but firmly, "We have him." Graham had come for him, to help him, and he had gone willingly. I was so relieved. He told me that Martin was mending and adjusting to his spirit body. I asked why he had died just when he'd finally found happiness in his life. It seemed so unfair. My friend put his head to one side as if listening to someone and then turned back to me saying, "It was Martin's path to find happiness but not to live it." I was so sad. I didn't want to hear this. I asked, "Why would somebody choose that for themselves?" He just smiled kindly and said it was Martin's choice and that one day I would understand totally.

He told me to look at the flowers around the garden. I could see that there were hundreds, so beautiful, the colours mingled into each other - it was a lovely sight. He told me that every flower in this garden related to someone I had helped at some time in my life, and that it was entirely my choice to do so. Some of those times had been very painful for me, but again it was my choice. He emphasised that we always have a choice even though we may think otherwise. He pointed to the left where there were two huge roses, standing very tall and beautiful. They were perfect, one red and the other white. He told me that these were from my two brothers, who thanked me for all I had done for them. I felt numb, crushingly sad. I so wanted to see them, to hug them and feel their physical presence. He knew this and he stepped forward, folding his arms around me. The love spilled over. There are no words.

At that moment I was aware of being back in the churchyard, sitting on the bench with tears streaming down my cheeks. How embarrassing. I quickly wiped them away with my sleeve. There were two ladies standing in front of Graham's memorial stone, one older and the other younger, holding her arm. They looked at me, concerned. I sniffed in a rather unladylike way, took a deep breath and walked over to them to say hello. The older lady pointed out that the person on the headstone was not very old, so I told her it was my brother Graham and that I had just lost another brother. The older lady told me that her sister had recently died and she missed her terribly. Her friend said that she was so upset that they were going to see "One of those medium people." Talk about an opener! I thought spirit can't be serious – now, in front of the church? But then again, why not? It was very fitting. I took the lady's hand and said to her, "I am one of those medium people, may I speak with you?" She said, "Oh, please do."

As soon as she said this, I was aware of spirit gathering around her to bring love, support and guidance to ease her aching soul. I gave her details of who had come to speak to her - her family, her sister - and she cried tears of joy. It only took ten minutes and at the end of it she said, "I don't know who you are, but thank you, everything has changed. You're an angel and I'll remember this all my life."

When the ladies turned and walked away from me, I smiled and realised that this had been a powerful and beautiful experience. At one of the lowest points of my life, when I wanted to hide and growl, I still had the capacity for such love to help someone else in a time of awful pain. Even when I had thought that all my strength was gone, I had become stronger and I thanked the spirit world for it. It humbled me and I loved them even more. I have never seen that lady since but when I go to the churchyard now I think of her and wish her well; although, that said, I'm not sure which one of us was the angel.

Martin was cremated in a white coffin - he would have liked that. The funeral was well attended and Andy came over from America. We played September Blue as we had done at Graham's funeral; he had also passed in September, so it was going to be a tough month every year from then on. I spoke at the funeral, which was very difficult, but I did it for him and I did it well. Where did I find the strength? The vicar told me I didn't have to speak if it was too much for me, and that was like a red rag to a bull. I would never have allowed anyone else to speak for him. I have never shirked my responsibilities to my brothers. I know he was there listening and joining in with us. And I know he's at peace. I too have found a certain peace with letting him go to continue his journey.[2]

---

[2] I wrote this chapter on the first anniversary of his passing. I still love and miss him.

CHAPTER NINE

Friends

I hadn't known anyone like him before, nor have I since.
He was a man of extremes, he loved to shock with his language
and his foibles – and although I'm unshockable, he did try.
He had a warm sense of humour, but could be so
cantankerous and stubborn.

My friend Martin was a lovely chap who would make me laugh, and I learned pretty quickly that it was an honour to know him. He taught me so much.

It was a Sunday morning in March and I was cooking in the kitchen. I had promised my husband a roast dinner, so was busy preparing vegetables when the `phone rang. A gentleman's voice, or rather what sounded like the voice of a gentle man, echoed down the `phone asking for someone whom I didn't know. He was adamant that he had the correct number and I remembered my husband's moan the night before about some bloke who kept calling despite telling him he had the wrong number. I listened patiently. He had a very lovely, beautifully enunciated voice and it somehow made me smile listening to him; he was eager to contact a friend who had worked for Age Concern and used to visit him at his home. I asked him if he had an address for his friend. When he gave me the information, I realised that it was across the other side of town. He obviously had the wrong number but was very insistent that I help him. Somewhat bemused I agreed to try to

find his friend and ring him back. I left the house with the beef cooking
- the aromas making me hungry - and drove across town to find this
address.

I rang the doorbell and a small, round lady with a very kind face answered. She thanked me for coming, but said she no longer worked at
Age Concern and was not in a position to be able visit the man. She
assured me he was a lovely man, an author named Martin, and he was
quite lonely. On reaching home, I called him and told him what she had
said. He didn't speak. I was just going to say goodbye when he asked,
"Will you come and visit me?" I was a bit taken aback by this and for a
few seconds didn't know what to say. But then I heard myself saying,
"Of course, where do you live?"

The following Thursday, as agreed, I found my way to the address
I'd been given, an unassuming apartment block a few minutes away
from where I lived. Martin had given me the code needed to enter the
outer door of the block. I walked up to the third floor where his door
was ajar, so I went in. Martin was sitting in a chair in the lounge, with
one arm in a sling; I never did find out why he wore it - he told me a
different story every time I asked, but he was never without it. He spoke
with gusto and I liked him instantly. It soon became clear that he was a
real character, very bohemian with a brilliant long term memory and
absolutely no short term memory. That would be something to do with
the alcohol then! By his own admission, he was an alcoholic; it was his
way of coping.

The room he sat in was untidy and the furniture sparse and worn. I
felt a compulsion to clean and vacuum for him, which I did regularly,
but he always told me off and asked me to come and talk with him.
Some of the things he talked about brought such sadness to my heart -
he told me about his father's suicide after the war and how he had links
with family all over Europe. His most passionate subjects were his wife
and his daughter. His wife had died of cancer and he had loved her so
much and missed her every day. He talked of his 'coup de foudre' - love
at first sight. His daughter lived in Italy, where he had also lived,
teaching English. He was fluent in a few European languages and was,
in lucid moments, a very intelligent man.

He would continuously smoke roll-ups and then throw them mindlessly over the back of the chair when he was finished! There would always be a small pile of ash behind his chair. The drink was his crutch, continuously all day. For all this, he was a lovely man and I thoroughly enjoyed being in his company even though he was a little eccentric. I loved him from day one. He made me laugh so much, although he did tell the same story again and again as he couldn't remember that he'd already told me five minutes earlier. I just sat and listened each time, my expression as it was the first time I'd heard it. He'd attended RADA when he was young but had wanted to write, not to act. Indeed he did write a series of three books about owls; he always likened himself to an owl - free spirited and soaring.

I used to visit once or twice a week and it was never a chore. I hadn't known anyone like him before, nor have I since. He was a man of extremes, he loved to shock with his language and his foibles – and although I am unshockable, he did try. He had a warm sense of humour, but could be so cantankerous and stubborn, especially when it came to eating. He was just getting thinner and although I made and bought him food he still ate very little. As time went on his memory just seemed to get worse and I could see that this was for his own benefit. So much painful information spilled out of him.

One night I had a call to inform me that he'd been found in the flat after falling and had lain in the same place for twenty-four hours. It was heart-breaking to hear this. I went to the hospital to see him and he hated it there. But it was clear he could no longer go back to the flat, so a place was found for him at a local nursing home. He was such a bad boy there and the nurses were despairing of him. He insisted on smoking in his room and anywhere else that took his fancy because no-one was going to tell him what to do. He was such a free spirit.

One night I went to visit and he was in a lot of pain and sweating profusely. Everywhere in his body ached and the look on his face said it all. He was rocking and moaning, so I read to him from a poetry book I'd bought for him. The next thing I knew he was back in hospital after another fall and was in a lot of pain, grabbing the bedclothes and pulling them down, pointing to his stomach where something was hurting.

Next day I knew I just had to see him. His daughter was on her way back from Italy. The sun was shining brightly through the window as I sat down. He was unconscious and on a morphine driver by this time and I knew he was very poorly. His white beard clung roughly to his chin and his grey hair fell lamely around his forehead, his nails and fingers yellow and ridged through smoking. He looked restful but much older than his sixty or so years. As I stared at him, I wondered why I had received that wrong number `phone call just a year before - surely it had been no accident. Now I just sat for an hour wishing him peace and holding his hand, letting him know someone was close. I was the last to see him alive. Martin died that day before his daughter could get here.

He had told me some months earlier that I should write a book and that he would help me. My first instinct was to laugh - that was not going to happen! But I've been aware of him so much since he passed and have seen him in my mind's eye, so well, fit and handsome.

He was passionate for so much - his writing, his love, his family – and he taught me about passion for life. He told me that every day you should realise the most amazing possibilities your life can offer, for you are limited only by your own imagination. In amazing moments of lucidity, he gave me the most amazing insights to life and to visions where I could only dream of treading. When he orated he held me in his sway and I owe a debt of gratitude for meeting him.

I sometimes wonder... if I had not been there to answer that call, or if I had been in a different mood, what would I have missed out on? There is always a reason why people come and go in our lives, so let's give thanks for knowing them. Some cannot stay too long on this Earth. How many people who come into our lives become friends? Why some and not others? How many of us have had friends, only to find out that they've had their own agenda all along, and have been using us for their own ends? I know that I have. But let's not be bitter or angry - we've done a service. However we feel, it's a shame to pass up on an opportunity of friendship. I know I'm lucky to have a handful of friends who know the real me and love me for who I am, and I know I could call on any of them at any time even if I haven't see them for months on end. We all link together one way or another and there's always a higher purpose to friendships. I could not have written this book without mentioning Martin, because of the strange way we came to be in each other's lives and how much I learned from him.

I like to be there for other people, particularly in the spiritual sense, and they are friends as we are all connected. Then again, I have some friends that, due to my commitments, I cannot get to see as often I would like to and some get very upset with me. It's a fine line to walk, a balance you have to find. You can't work for spirit without other people helping you in the first place, but not all people will become close friends, or will need to be friends at all. It may be your path to assist just a little and then walk away. Sometimes that can be misunderstood, or seen as aloofness. So it's important to be aware of how our actions affect others. It hurts to feel rejected, as I'm sure you know. We need to be aware of ourselves and how our relationships benefit one another. Sometimes we are just not meant to be together. However, we always have many people in the spirit world who are there for us, no matter where we go and what we do. We are never alone - although that doesn't compensate for a warm hug when we need one!

CHAPTER TEN

Spirit All the Way

"I pledge my honour that Spiritism is true and I know that Spiritism is infinitely more important than literature, art, politics and in fact anything in the world." Sir Arthur Conan Doyle

I don't have all the answers to all the questions people ask. Sometimes we have to find the answers for ourselves - not everything can be given to us. I will always share what the spirit world deems to share with me because that's what I'm here to do. I don't worry about it so much now. Nor do I worry about minor details in life such as the full ironing basket, or a floor that needs cleaning!

As long as I can remember I have heard voices, but I used to think that it was me talking with myself. Realising the truth was a very gradual process. I was being taught an understanding, a greater knowledge. There is so much more than this world, much more than we can fathom, and there are still great discoveries to be unearthed, amazing facts to be found that will lead us all on a journey far beyond our current limits. It may even be you who finds them... You have to look, to try and to trust. I know how difficult it is to believe in yourself when you never had anyone else believe in you, when you have always been the one sitting in the corner, staying in the shadows, always watching. How do we not realise we are just as important as anyone else, with our own purpose?

I have been asked many times, "How do you speak to the spirit world?" Often it's not a physical hearing but a voice that's heard in my head. It is very clear and precise, and it's definitely not mine. It's the 'knowing' that makes it different and that took a long time for me to find. Sometimes a sitter has asked, "Can you just bring my Dad here for me? I'd like a chat with him." Or they've said, "I don't want to speak to them, send them back." Well, it's certainly not up to me who comes forward from the spirit world, as they always bring just what you need. I always attempt to bring forward the communicator and personal details of the person I am talking with, to prove their continuous existence in the spirit world, and to explain why they have come with a message. It is not up to me to order anyone to step forward. They come because you need that particular energy at that particular time. In my experience it will always be the one who is needed to help you that will come.

Even when there is an interest in working for the spirit world, it's not easy to believe that it's spirit talking to you. This may be because people think they are not 'worthy'. Of course you are! How could you not be? You are spirit too. Others, who really do want to work for spirit, fear that it's their imagination, so they move away from it. But if you trust in the power of you, and the power of the love that comes to you (knowing you are worthy), the possibilities can be endless.

There are so many ways of working spiritually. Clairvoyance is clear seeing; clairaudience is clear hearing; clairsentience is clear sensing. Some mediums use one of these, some use more, and it varies according to the individual and how the energy that works with you wishes to use you at the time of the contact. It is a subtle and divine force that exists within all of us, waiting to be tapped into. When the time is right for me to assist someone, I use the relevant area as easily as switching on a light. My senses become heightened and through emotion, feelings and sight I will sense the world of spirit. When you feel this energy you will not want to let it go - it feels so good! So let it flow through every part of you until you and spirit are one, joined by threads of love and hope.

When I am working, how the message is brought depends on who I am working with; that goes for the people here and the people over there. It also depends on me. Messages can be clear and succinct or some can come to me in an abstract form. All show guidance and bring forward absolute proof. It follows, then, that we need to watch for signs through coincidences and daily events. There is no such thing as coincidence and random déjà-vu, it is always by design. Your soul has a role to play and you are so much more than the circumstances and events in your life.

Everyone has helpers who work alongside us in the spirit world, no matter what we do and who we are. There are no exceptions. You can never be alone, even if you try! You are a spiritual being having an Earthly experience. That is a very important piece of information. Such self-discovery is necessary for moving beyond your Earthly fears and connecting with your loved ones, with true spiritual communion. The people who commune with me in the spirit world are all very different. I don't yet know them all, and it did take quite a time to recognise them, but I didn't need to know their identities, just trust them. They switch and change from time to time, as my (and their) needs change; but we give each other endless blessings and they always allow me to sway in the winds, to dance my dance, to sing my songs, and love me nonetheless. The Chinese gentleman, whom I have been aware of for so long, knows me very well. He is patient with me, loves me, and cajoles me to be courageous and strong. He helps me find my own destiny, encouraging me to look within to find the chrysalis waiting. He helps me listen to the beautiful guidance held deep inside, waiting for me whenever I need it. He does, however, sometimes raise his eyebrows at me in a despairing sort of way, when I make a complete mess of things - oh yes, I do that frequently! Then there is a gentleman with a big black hat who barks his instructions at me in an 'I can say anything and you must obey me!' sort of way. I always do. Then there is Queen Victoria… I will tell you more about her later.

You need to allow yourself to be a little vulnerable. You have to give yourself over to trust in spirit. In that moment when you stand tall and stand up to be counted, no matter what it is, the spirit world will never let you down.

I am who I am, and I make no excuses or apologies. I am very earthy. I treat everyone in the same way whoever they are. I've been told by complete strangers, "You always seem to have that knack of being able to relate to anyone." It is no effort, it is just me, although I am told it is a gift. Indeed, I have not always thought of it like that; sometimes I want to be angry, I don't want to love. I allow Earthly situations to overwhelm me and that is not always positive. Most of the time, though, I'd like to wrap everyone up in angel wings of love and light!

I have chosen this pathway for the reason that I'm able to use the ever present universal energy with some ease - or at least that's how it looks. You will never know the hours of work I have laboured to hone that spiritual connection, to access the infinite libraries of wisdom that are shown to me by my spirit friends daily. I have put in hours of experience, tears, pain, laughter and love. I have listened to my heart and doubted it. I have suffered tears and anguish and lack of self-worth. That said, I don't regret one second of it.

The way that messages are received from spirit seems to be different for every medium. I suppose it's a bit like someone playing Pictionary in your head, with a little bit of charades thrown in while someone is talking to you on the telephone. There's a massive amount of mixed signals, which have to be received and interpreted very quickly. It has to be fine-tuned. It has to be so good that a melody can be heard clearly and succinctly. Each worker has their own code, their own way of linking with the energies and images that are brought in, but the message will always be of love. That should always be felt in the heart, the true seat of power within the body. There will be no negativity in the words. If this is the case then they are not from spirit, because they know our fears and will not frighten us. They understand how vulnerable we are and they know how much courage some people need to display to reach them. They will not inform us of worrying information, such as if someone is going to die unexpectedly. It's surprising how many people say to me that they can't have a reading because it's 'too scary'. No medium worth his or her salt, and who connects with the purely positive energy of the vibrational realms, should give any negative details.

The spirit world completely understands that my intention is to bring the endless blessings that will unite a finite love to an infinite love. Prior to any communication, I always request only to receive and give to whoever really needs it most. Unfortunately, we here on Earth have a different perception of 'need'. Some people think they need it more than others, but we cannot know; we are not walking in anyone else's shoes, so how can we know their life? Only those in the spirit world understand the real help that is needed and when to send it. Even in our darkest times, somehow we shall always have access to a switch to illuminate our world with diamond bright light. Most of us know where it is, we are just afraid to press the switch...

We all need support now and again. It is sometimes difficult to be ourselves and surrender to who we are, to embrace the love connection within us and heal our own wounds. Who better to give that extraordinary divine intervention, bringing hope and promise to you, than someone who loves you and who knows you well? When you receive a correct spirit message, your heart will understand the beautiful energy that consciously connects to you and around you. It is as important to feel the message as it is to hear it. Love transcends all planes of living and levels of energy right through to your heart. Your loved ones long to tell you that they love you, that they are here every day, and you are not alone.

I always know when I have a good connection with the spiritual energies. Why don't you try for yourself and see how it feels? It helps if you have an open mind and start in a relaxed state, not sitting with crossed arms or legs, not too emotional or scared. Such things affect the energy around you. Don't try and force anything to happen and just see what transpires. Look for the peace inside - where the real you is. Who holds the key to that door? You do of course! So go and unlock it and find your amazing potential to live however you wish on this planet. The possibilities are endless, with the boundless positive energies which wrap around you like angel wings. Look within and you will never go without. We all work with energy, whether we know it or not. It is multi-dimensional, connected to an eternal being that has love at its core and has no beginning or end. It sounds pretty big doesn't it? It is! Indeed, we have different energies all around us relating to different levels - emotional, physical and spiritual. Most of us have those strange perceptions from time to time, such as the feeling in the pit of your stomach when you know something is wrong. Are you focussing on the negative or is it something else? Look inside yourself for the intuition that will allow you to open your heart and your mind, and which can unlock your reality. But what is this energy, and where does it come from? Someone once explained to me that it is what makes the sun shine and the grass grow. I liked that – simple, unquestioning and easy to accept. Sometimes we do not need to know everything, it's enough to realise that it makes us feel warm and precious, like a child's laugh.

Consciously give yourself to this connection. Feel the warmth and the power as you and spirit are indeed one. Take as much as you want. That power is free for all who search for it, linked with the invisible strands of love to help us on our paths. It's the sacred journey that's important. The spirit world is with us no matter what we do; no matter who we are. Spirit does not condemn or judge; they know that we already do enough to hurt ourselves and each other. I believe that no matter what standing you have on this Earth plane, you are equal to everyone else. Equality is not about the trappings of wealth and fame, or lack of them, or whatever human attachments you may make. There is one basic rule, that we are all deserving of love - every single one of us. That's it in a nutshell. No matter what our religious knowledge or beliefs, we all have access to a gateway on something much more powerful than ourselves.

To walk the path of working for spirit is difficult. Our physical lives are affected by the changes needed, and some of that can be painful. On this path, some are sure-footed and some are not; then there are gaps in between. That's where the love is, it's the glue that holds it all together, that binds us all together. It needs to be discovered, so we need to let down our guard and trust in the new shoots that appear in our lives. Sometimes we can't see them due to the stressful situations we find ourselves in. We may hate it, not want it, so we need to detach a little and see what transpires, see what we need to do.

Sometimes it's hard to find a 'healthy medium'! We sometimes give too much. I have known of working mediums, both novice and experienced, who fall ill or become unbalanced due to the work that they do. Indeed, to work for the spirit world you have to have complete focus, trust, the best intention, and be completely dedicated to what you do. It is common sense that our energy fields can be affected, so we have to make sure we receive back energy into our lives and balance the work we do, as too much giving can devalue it. A vast amount of any medium's time is spent travelling around the country to various services or appointments. True spirit workers love to help people find their solutions to their problems by giving hope. They know without doubt that the spirit world exists and that we all need that love connection, physically and spiritually, and we should never give up trying for that. But it can get very tiring physically and, indeed, I have often been reprimanded by people for working relentlessly for spirit, seven days a week sometimes. I just can't turn people away.

I am very lucky to have an understanding husband who, despite the fact that he doesn't believe what I believe, still supports me regardless. He knows it's my choice. I have seen many relationships affected by this work but it's our own choice how we cope with it. We do need to be firmly grounded. We need to eat properly. The hours can be unsocial and we have to fit things in alongside the day job, the one that pays the mortgage. This can be very difficult for some, but how much do you want it? In fact how much effort is anything you really want worth? There has to be balance in all life - yin and yang, black and white, right and wrong, cause and effect. It is the spiritual law.

However, you don't have to be a medium to be working for spirit. Many people on this Earth work for the spiritual realms daily and have no idea that they are doing so. It is not just about giving messages or spiritual communication. The key is healing, loving, caring, supporting and giving of your time, your love and your energy for others. How about a helping hand here? Make a cup of tea there? Many people in this world need that love, care and guidance in this world. Many are very alone, scared and frightened of living. In this day of miracles there should be no-one alone, there should be no-one suffering, yet there may be someone in need closer than we think. We can all be part of a beautiful spiritual army, linking together, helping others to progress in their lives, helping them to be the best they can be. There will be a knock-on effect of moving us forward in ours too.

I don't have readings myself, or rarely do, and I don't like to go to services or demonstrations of mediumship because I become irritated. I know I'm not alone in this. In such situations, I find I'm receiving information messages too and I can't give them to people - so I keep away. But I do like to read old spiritual books and about spiritual philosophy. There have been some great authors. Arthur Findlay's books, such as The Edge of the Etheric, and indeed Sir Arthur Conan Doyle's writings, are important. I hold many of the old mediums of the past in great esteem, such as Bertha Harris, whose book fell on my head from a shelf above me as I walked past! We will never know everything but it's fun to search and look at the stories of life and of spirit, and try to understand what it's all about. Many years ago, spiritual philosophy was widely taught and read in development circles. It helped us gain that deeper understanding of what we all are. It does seem that this is diminishing now, as the attention to this in spiritual meetings is not of the quality it once was. Most people would rather just have messages from their families and loved ones, which I suppose is understandable. The people who need more will search for more. When the time is right, it will come, it shall be given.

Indeed we are all philosophers in some way. We can all tell a life story which had a consequence, but how many of us actually learn from it? How many move on from it and make it part of our armoury? Instead, many seem to carry it around like a burden. I didn't used to like talking philosophy at all and found it difficult to talk about my past and feelings, but I now consider myself very lucky to have someone who has helped me to overcome those blockages which I set for myself. Spirit continues to work with me for the philosophy, but they want me to keep it earthy and simple.

I am aware of people who have sat in development circles for six months and then insist they can work as mediums in Spiritualist churches and give private readings. But there is no quick fix. Some people do it, they get ill and then they stop and wonder, "Why has spirit done this to me?" They don't realise that they have tried to run before they can walk. They don't see that it is their own responsibility. They have done this to themselves, through desire, impatience or greed. We make our own choices. So we must make peace in and with our own lives and then hopefully we can have a positive effect on others' lives. Even if the intention is good, it still takes time.

The quality of spiritual communication and connection is paramount to me. Anyone is only as good as their last message! The trouble is that some people are just too accepting, and some believe without prejudice that what they are being given is gospel. They want the communication from their loved ones so much. There are practising mediums who give no mention of the communicator who is bringing the message, yet we are supposed to prove the existence of the spirit world. I think that sort of detail is pretty necessary, but you'd be amazed how many don't. Everyone should question the message they're receiving and, if it doesn't feel right, say so. That is how we mediums learn to move forward. No-one is infallible, but the spirit world does want your message to be correct for you. All of us Earthly mediums work for the same boss - we are a spiritual army. All of us around the world work tirelessly to bring that love to you - all it takes is for you to embrace it. The medium is just the middle person. The important facts are you and your loved one. It should be all about the love.

Ego is a very small word with a very large effect. Our ego is there all the time and, for most of us, it tells us who we are and what we deem to be. We amble through life and do not always use our knowledge for positive effect; it can turn ugly, and we have all been on the receiving end of that sometimes in our lives. There are always consequences and then a life becomes rocked with negativity and we get hurt. Then ego raises its head higher over the parapet, causing jealousy, envy, fear and anger. We must try to look within as it is only we who are to blame. We must never fall for the illusions of ego because most of the time it leads to negativity. We mustn't listen to people who are trying to drag us into pointless situations by feeding our ego. We know it will end in heartbreak and pain. We just need to be who we truly are, in all our loveliness. If people don't like us or don't agree with us, then the problem is invariably not ours but theirs. Send them a happy thought and let it go;

spirit will do the rest in helping you to stay in the light. When we have a problem we can try to change the way we look at it. It is not good or bad, it just is. We can try to realise that all that has happened is simply a part of our make-up, to get us here to this point. We must ask ourselves, "What are they trying to tell me?" then wrap our arms around ourselves and know that spirit is holding us safe.

Throughout our lives, we can ask spirit for guidance and it will be given without fail. Angels, helpers or guides - whatever we want to label them - are only too happy to help us. We just need to ask. Did you know that every thought we think is a real entity, and every thought is heard? I explain it like this: we all have an invisible team who sit around, having a cuppa, playing cards and not doing much... so tell them what help you need. They can help us to manifest miracles in our lives if we only give them the chance. Spirit knows when we need help and when we need to overcome difficult obstacles and challenges ourselves, but we still have to make the choices and voice it. It makes it final then, doesn't it? Try to say it out loud.

Spirit cannot, and will not, tell us what to do - because it's our life, our journey, our choices. They will not tell us what our future will be, as life is shifting and changing every day. We change it by the decisions we make. Tomorrow we will change our minds, so the direction changes again. The destination is written but the journey is not, and the pathway is just what we make it. It is very challenging sometimes, and very beautiful at other times. We create and choose our own Heaven or our own Hell here on Earth. It's like the choice between taking the motorway or the back roads, the escalator or the stairs. You choose how you get to your destination and you can make it as fun or gloomy as you like. So be happy, for goodness sake!

I must assure you that spirit can never hurt you. Many people believe they can and I've been called to several places where there are 'strange goings-on' - houses, work places and nightclubs. This is one aspect of my work I keep to myself, as I find it very personal. I go there purely to help them and I will talk to spirit but I won't chase them around. That's not respectful. Sometimes, indeed there are spooky goings-on, but it's not a bad thing. It's just that help is needed for people who are stuck between one world and another, people who are just confused and can't move on. Yes, we all get confused, on both sides. I just try to help them overcome their blockage – that's if they want to, because we can't force any spirit to go anywhere they don't want to go.

It does seem that when the uninitiated sense the presence of someone from the spirit world it is immediately taken as a bad vibration, whether anything is visible, audible or not. Indeed, it seems alien. But it's important to keep calm and not react for the sake of it - it's the fear that usually does the damage. Yes, there are mischievous spirits but we can usually reason it out and help them across. The spirit world does like to get our attention, by moving items, making noises or making you feel cold, particularly at sensitive moments in our lives. But don't be concerned, they just want to be noticed and acknowledged - so we should do that. It may be someone we know. They are still the same as when they were on Earth, so they want to be included. And if we don't know them, then we should show a little kindness because they may not have had any of that for a long time. They come because we can sense them and we may be the only one in the house who can. Imagine that - being invisible for years and then getting someone who can sense them or see them; should we blame them for causing a rumpus sometimes?

I have to say that I have never come across any spirit who is evil. I don't like that word but it does the job. I have come across some unhappy ones, mischievous and playful ones, and downright awkward ones, but they can't hurt us. They can't always understand where they are or what they're doing; so we have a chat and discuss where they need to be, and what their options are. All they need is respect and love, and that's exactly what we would expect our loved ones to receive, regardless of who they managed to contact. It's just a matter of understanding and knowledge, a little beyond this world.

I once did a 'clearing' with a couple of friends at some apartments with upper and lower floors, where a young couple lived on the ground floor. It was quite a rough area and when I arrived I wondered where spirit had sent me. We went in and there were the young couple with their son. The front of the flat was no problem, but going through to the rear of the property we found the energy was really strong. Whenever I do this, a small group of spirit people always walk in with me to assist. We worked together in a small space. Truly, I have never felt anything like it. We were able to 'send over' the lady who was causing the problems; this was Margaret, who had lived in the apartment for many years. Then we continued, as spirit requested, and it went quiet. But suddenly it seemed that many souls were starting to walk forward, searching for the light, stuck in this area with much sadness and pain. We worked for quite a while in this building, and it was beautiful to help these people across. When we had finished I informed the couple it should be a lot quieter, and then I drove home exhausted. I slept for eighteen hours the following day. Later I had a call from the gentleman who lived there who told me that all was now quiet; he thanked me profusely for going and said he had come across my number by chance. I thanked spirit. After all, I am just the instrument, and spirit plays the tune.

One of the most terrible experiences in this world is to lose a child. I have seen the aftermath and it tears your heart out. But I have had the privilege of bringing through proof of survival of their children to parents and it is the most beautiful of connections, and often the strongest. It's difficult for the layman to understand a Spiritualist's thoughts on this - that we are here of our choosing to experience all we need to on a soul level, and then we simply go home. Some people talk of the Earth as a school, but I don't like that description; to me that would mean that we've been sent here to suffer and to learn. An ever-loving God would never allow us to suffer involuntarily and we are never sent. We only choose. We need to know that we are just remembering the right pieces of information at the right time. However we may doubt it, there is always a plan.

CHAPTER ELEVEN

The Link

*The spirit world is my reason for living, my food, my life. They
hold my love for them in the palm of their hand and they love
me in return unconditionally. I only hope I can honour
them enough… and live up to expectations.*

My friendly spirit workers know me very well. They know how to push
my buttons and put me in situations that spur me on to greater heights.
They have done so many times and I try hard to do this for others, here
and now, and bring them what they need. I always meet everyone with
the same warm hug as I know that everyone needs that connection.
Whether you know it or not, your spirit connection is ever-changing
and evolving into something wonderful for this world right here, right
now. All is just as it is meant to be. This is spiritual alchemy.

I feel completely different to how I did when I was a child because I
have no more fear. I have faced and overcome it. It's true that my fear took
years to eradicate, but experience by experience it waned and my understanding grew. Occasionally I wobble and feel that I am inadequate for my
pathway. Fear and doubt are awful - they can consume you if you take too
much notice of them and I don't want to be scared of life or death anymore. Most of the time it's the idea of fear that causes the problem, not an
actual act; so let's feel the fear and do it anyway, and we may find that it's
not nearly as bad as we think. (I still have my fear of heights to contend
with, which is not as nearly as bad as the very long list I used to have.)

We are all here for a reason and we are all born to shine in our own respective lives. Consciously or unconsciously we give people around us permission to do the same throughout our lives, including our children, our families and sometimes even people we don't know very well. We often find it easier to help others with their fears than to do it for ourselves. That's because of the effort involved. But there's no time like the present is there? Tomorrow will not be the same as today and the opportunity may not be available to you then.

I use the term 'spirit' all the time in this book and this relates to all the spiritual people and energy in and from the spirit world; all of us have the same energy. However, on this plane of life many people use the words spiritual and spirituality as general terms that cover a broad range of characteristics. Spiritual means caring and understanding, giving and loving, aware of something more, much greater than us. But not everyone who calls themselves spiritual actually is that way, and we all know someone like this. All we can do is wish them well, hope they find their path and keep their nose out of our business and concentrate on their own spirit. Where does the true beauty lie? The real person is an essence that resides within; we know who we are, and we can always try to be more.

People often remark, "So you don't believe in God, then?" That makes me both smile and feel irritated in equal measures - of course I do. He means the world to me, literally. Maybe I don't see Him how others do; we all have our own ways of seeing and no way is wrong. After all, we are all linked by love and matter in this world and we shall all go to the same place in the next, whatever label you wish to give it. These days the G-word seems to have become one that people deny and are embarrassed about. I find that very sad. The word 'church' has the same effect for many, particularly the young. Why is that? What's the problem with attending a church if you wish to? It doesn't matter what denomination. And you can see your God however you wish Him, Her or It to be, however it slots into your life. They can be with you anywhere, they listen and assist you and are always there. Truly, God and spirit can be completely relied on - more so than anyone we know here on Earth.

So why is this not recognised? It may be because if we do start to think about God, then we shall have to start to look at ourselves… "Oh no, don't go there!" I know this because I used to do the same thing. I would run in the other direction at any mention of the words 'religion' or 'spiritual', and I'm almost ashamed to admit that I referred to someone on more than one occasion as 'a religious freak'. But I have learned that it's not about religion, but spirituality - the spiritual person within, who is capable of much love, kindness, growth and truth.

So we have the big G and we have spirits who, like us, have had a planetary experience and have come back to help us. We also have angels who watch over us - they are the messengers and protectors. We have the masters, enlightened beings who oversee world development and plane-tary evolution. In the spirit world they preside over the spirit schools, having complete humility and love. Lastly in the chain there is us, placed in this physical body to have this experience that we call 'life' - some good, some not so good, some ambling through, exercising our free will every day. Not everyone wants to know this truth so we can only share it with those who are prepared to listen and to expand their spirituality.

My husband often tells me he is going 'stokin', which always makes me laugh. I tell him there is no Hell beyond this life, we are in it now. This is what the spirit world often tells me. To them, we are dead and they are living - after all, they're not in pain, they don't have a physical body and they can go where they like. I think they have a point. Yet there are many levels within the spirit world and each is very different. Where we go to when we die entirely depends on what we have learned here. So the ball really is in our court; where do we want to be?

I want to relate a conversation I had with Graham, a while after he had died. On a regular basis, I sit quietly to go within as that is where the peace and calm can be found and that is where we find the beautiful connection. I was attempting to do this one evening. As usual, the day had been hectic, I had so much flitting around my head and there was much to do. I'd had a particularly trying day at work - some people can be mean. I was self-doubting and wanted to climb into a big hole. I switched off all the `phones, locked the door and asked to be left alone. Concentrating on breathing deeply, I started to relax…

I was standing in a beautiful cornfield, interlaced with bright red poppies and sunflowers. The field was on an incline and ahead in the centre was a huge tree which seemed to reach to the heavens. I felt the sensations. It was warm, with a gentle breeze, and the sky had somewhat strange colours - blue and pink striped, interspersed with yellow blotches. As I turned and looked beyond the field, I realised that the land on either side went down to a valley and I was standing much higher that I had realised. The whole scene felt entirely natural, there was no fear. I suddenly knew that I had to make my way up the field to the tree. As I strode through the field, the poppies danced and tickled my legs while the sunflowers, which were all the same height as my face, seemed to lean into me lilting a silent tune. Every flower was perfect and the bloodiest red and brightest sunshine yellow. I marvelled at the wondrous sight of nature. It took a while to reach the tree and as I approached it I could study its details. It was very old and tall, the bark dry, and at the base of the trunk, which must have been about eight feet in circumference, the root tendrils pushed through the dry and dusty ground. I started to walk around the tree holding out my arm and allowing my fingertips to trail over the bark as I walked the circle. When I completed it, I turned to gaze across the fields - the incline seemed to go on for ever, each field a different colour, each containing something different.

It was then I heard his voice. "Jac?" I swung round to see him standing there in exactly the clothes he'd been buried in – an orange sweatshirt and black Nike trousers. He looked very well and had an ear-to-ear smile. I launched myself at him and he laughed a gentle throaty laugh and hugged me with fervour. I had a lump in my throat could barely speak; all I could mutter was "How? Why?" He released me, walked forward a few feet and motioned for me to sit in the grass surrounded by the poppies. He looked amazing and his blue eyes were twinkling.

It just seemed so normal to be with him right there, right then. He told me that he'd chosen this place to meet me and that I could always see this place in my mind and he would be there. He wanted me to have that. He told me he'd returned many times to see everyone, particularly Mum, and I said I would tell her. He related details of my life that he knew were occurring, very thoughtful as he spoke, almost as if he were partly elsewhere. I asked him how he was and he told me he was well, happy and content. When he had passed, he'd found it difficult initially. He'd awoken in a place that was all mirrored, at least that's how it seemed to him. But then he'd realised it wasn't a mirror but 'something else I can't quite describe' and he smiled. He didn't want to elaborate; I don't think he could find the words and I didn't press him. He went on to say that he'd been met by our grandmother when he passed, and he had heard me and trusted my words because he was already partly in the spirit world. I felt my vision blurring with the welling tears. "It really is true," he told me, "you do see everyone who has gone before and you do see yourself for who you really are." His eyes were so blue, deep and wise.

Then he asked me to listen to him carefully. Our eyes locked and I felt sudden apprehension as something serious loomed. He told me that I was destined to work for spirit. It was to be a hard path but there would be many assisting me on the path I was treading. He continued, saying it was not just about me but about everyone else. I was quite confused, so he smiled and reassured me that I would have a better idea in time. He turned away and looked down the field. "Stop fighting it, Jac," he told me, "it's who you are." I knew what he meant. I'd been fighting the feeling forever. But how was I going to let it become a positive force when I believed it only ever caused me pain? It was as if he'd read my mind. "You have a rare gift, sis."

I held my sides as I fell around laughing. What was happening? I felt shocked, not believing that I was there. It was all too much at once. Then I thought, 'It's about time I got out of this. I need to go. This is way beyond my imagination.' But Graham continued, "There'll come a time when you'll work only for spirit; you'll fight it, but no matter what, it will be." I smiled and shook my head. He smiled back, ran his hand up the stem of a poppy and pulled the head towards him gazing at it. "I'll bring you red poppies every time you need to be reminded of this conversation, and yellow sunflowers for the light that continuously shines from your heart." We stood up and he held out his hand to steady me; it was warm and real. "You have to go back, we're done for now."

I panicked. Suddenly I wanted to stay with him, it seemed like no time at all together. He said, "Walk back the way you came, Jac." I asked, "Are we out of time already?" He smiled again. "There's no time where I am, so no, we could never be out of time. I know that's hard for you to understand but nothing has limits here. Everything is where and when it's meant to be." I hugged him - he was warm and solid, my brother. I told him, "Before I go, I have to say something to you. I'm sorry I switched off your life support. I hope I did right." He told me no apology was needed; it had been his time to go, and part of my path that I had to make the decision to do that. His mood suddenly lightened. "Gotta go, sis," he said, and pulled my arms from around him, raising his hand in salute as he walked slowly around the side of the tree and out of sight.

I stood very still, watching. I knew he'd gone. I did as I was told for a change, and ran down the field back to my starting point. Suddenly I jolted and felt very nauseous. Tears were streaming down my face; my heart felt heavy and was banging in my chest, and for a moment I was completely disorientated. I sobbed and it took ages for that feeling to go away. I was back. I had no idea what had just happened or how. I was just going to have five minutes' peace, but when I checked the clock an hour had passed. Was it real? Where had I been? I had to rationalise all that had just happened to me. I felt the overwhelming love he had for me, and the fact that I was the one to meet him, for whatever reason, humbled me to the core. I knew that I'd just had one of the first and most profound spiritual experiences of my life.

I had never related that story to anyone before. It's so personal. But I get it now, that it's not about me, it's about helping others to know that their very beloved family in spirit are right by their side. And it's true that poppies and sunflowers have been very prominent in my life, on a more or less day to day basis. The words or the pictures pop up whenever he wants me to know he's around, and I love him for it. It has helped me so much in some very dark situations and led me to find their resolution.

It was about five years before anything like this occurred again but this time under very different circumstances. By now my brother's words had come true and I'd been working flat out, busy all day in my day job and most nights working for spirit. Yes, I was tired but no more than usual, I was used to it. I had a job to do and they would help me do it. Then I awoke one Monday morning with the most awful dizziness. I had never experienced anything like this before, and the pain in my head was crippling. As I couldn't drive, and everyone else was at work, I asked Ernie to drive me to the doctor; he moaned at first, as usual, but he did. The doctor examined me, gave me a prescription, and told me to go back to bed, take the tablets and come back to see him in forty-eight hours if the symptoms persisted. I went home and stayed in bed for two days. After this time I felt worse, so I returned to the doctor on the Wednesday. At this point I could barely hold my head up; the light hurt my eyes and the dizziness was worse. He sent me to hospital. Ernie took me there, and then called Mum and my husband.

I truly don't remember much of what happened in the following two weeks. They put me in a private room and turned off the lights; the darkness was so soothing. I do remember the lumbar puncture - that really hurt! And I remember the opiates that made me heave my stomach up. But mainly I just slept and slept. For two weeks I was comatose, and then I suddenly woke up and felt fine.

Now, during that time away from my body, I'd had a ball. I'd been to a wonderful party, had meetings with people I didn't know and been aware of beings of light walking around me. I'd been half awake and half asleep, but I remember the party clearly. So many were present who had passed before - my brother, my grandparents, my Dad, and people I didn't know but who knew me. We laughed and chatted like it was just the most normal thing in the world. No mention of anything deep and meaningful, just laughter and fun. I could hear beautiful lyrical music. We were on the banks of a river by a castle and there were people in all sorts of strange clothes from the past and from the future. There was food, and it just seemed like everyone knew me and I was expected to know them.

It was there that I first saw a beautiful young lady, wearing a prominent hat with purple feathers and beautiful gloves with lace at the cuff. She looked awfully familiar, but I couldn't place her. Attentively, she told me it was time to go back and to pay attention to myself, as I was responsible for my physical body on the Earth. She gave me orders and instructions about what to look for and what I should be attending to. Her eyes curled playfully, gently admonishing me. Her demeanour was warm and knowing, but I saw a steel in her and knew that if she had been here on the Earth I would probably have avoided her. Then after two weeks I awoke and informed the doctors that I wanted to go home. They never really found anything major wrong with me - something to do with my sinuses and head, but not really defined. I knew something much deeper had occurred, much more than I was completely aware of. God knows, it felt like I was dying when I went into hospital and when I came out I felt refreshed, invigorated and really alive.

Now, something wonderful happened years later. My husband and I were invited to the Queen's Jubilee Garden Party, a real honour. We were very excited to say the least. A week or so before, I was in bed reading when I became aware of a presence in the bedroom. The same lady I had met at the party all that time before appeared next to me and I recognised her instantly. She was, I now understand, Queen Victoria. She seemed very pleased with herself, smiled at me and I smiled in return as she informed me that she knew I was going to the palace. I would walk through the palace then exit into the garden via double doors. I was to look to the left in the room before this. I told her I would, and she smiled and vanished. We went on the allotted day and it was beautifully sunny. While walking through Buckingham Palace I recalled her words, "Look to the left." And in the room on the wall to the left was a huge portrait of her, looking beautiful. I was humbled and smiled very self-indulgently; after all, no-one would have believed me if I'd told them. I had the best time of my life that day.

So what made me move from teaching and circles and Curry Club to working for spirit out there in the big wide world? I don't really know how it happened, it just did! This is the way things usually happen with me... before I realised, I was in the thick of it. Someone asked a small group of us to be the mediums at a church service one afternoon. I'll never forget the nausea in my stomach. I was dreading it - I couldn't speak in public! Still, I did it, and very well, and I have absolutely no idea how. When you stand up to work for spirit they will never let you down. It's we who lets ourselves down, if we don't put in the necessary work, time and effort for our pathway to succeed.

From that point on it all seemed to snowball very quickly. I would receive `phone calls asking me to work in many places, all by word of mouth. I was amazed where they led me and to whom they led me. It humbles me to think of some of the places that I've been taken to. For example, I've had a passion for castles and old buildings for as long as I can remember; there is something about the energy of those places that calls to me. Then in 2010 I had the opportunity to work in Warwick Castle, in the Grand Hall. This was one of the highlights of my life. It is a beautiful, enigmatic building, a place full of energy and not just with that of the living. To this day it is one of my favourite buildings and a wonderful place to work, and I thank my friend Clare who arranged both the events there.

The same day that I received the invitation to the Queen's garden party, I visited a local beauty spot called Stoneleigh Abbey, a few miles away from where I live. I'd been nursing my mother who'd had a shoulder operation a few days before, and my husband and I just wanted somewhere to go for a little respite. It's a lovely building, dating from the 12th century in places, and that day we joined a tour of the building. As I was walking around, I was aware of so many spirits whom I saw and heard. They seemed to want to attract my attention, and I heard less of the tour and more spiritual chatter. I know how spirit works, so I knew there was a reason for this. When the tour had finished, I went to ask if the manager was on site. My husband walked off in disgust and shook his head! The manager was indeed there, but how does one explain this? Paula studied me carefully and listened to what I had to say. I told her this was probably the strangest conversation she would have that day, but she didn't baulk, just asked me to email her my details and she would contact me if she wished to take it further. I emailed as soon as I arrived home and she replied the next day.

A few days later I went to the Abbey to read for her in the beautiful Orangery, which was the Summer House. Paula then had to go and lead a tour but asked me to return a little while later; when I did so, she told me that she was astounded at the amazing evidence I had passed on to her. (I am at pains to point out that none of this has anything to do with me; I am just the telephone, the spirit world uses me as I allow them to.) She asked me if I'd be willing to do some evening work to help them out, and I was only too pleased to oblige. I've been in the Abbey very late at night, in complete darkness, and it's wonderful - so many spirits from so many ages. It makes it even more special for me to know that Queen Victoria stayed there.

CHAPTER TWELVE

Physical Mediumship

To hear and see spirit standing before you is quite frankly mind-blowing, and to hear and see spirit via someone else on this Earth plane challenges all that you know and believe. It is so much more! So are you up to that challenge?

Physical mediumship takes understanding the realms of spirit to a completely different level. It becomes real and solid. It forces us to believe because we can see and feel the proof in this physical world. I heard about it when I began to attend the Spiritualist church many years ago and thought it sounded like something out of a science fiction novel. I didn't really believe it. Anyway, why would I purposely see such things when the spookies had caused me so much fear as a child? I'd have to be completely mad; there was no way I was going to attend anything like that, not a chance.

Well, gradually the desensitisation began. I was asked by a friend of mine to sit with her; we would sit in a darkened room with just a red light or a candle and her face would very clearly change into another. As we sat in the quiet, my heart would bang on my ribs in fear. One evening I was talking to my friend as she sat opposite me, obviously 'somewhere else'. Her head lolled to the side and the features were not hers. I very politely asked a question to see if there was any voice with this face, hoping not to get a reply, so I just sat and watched. Suddenly a man's voice boomed out of her very slowly: "Patience." It shook the room - and me, to the very core. I froze and didn't move a muscle for ages. That really shocked me, though she found it mildly amusing.

Another evening I was sitting quietly with her and my heart started to race. I felt very strange, my head became light, and the only way I can describe it is that it felt like someone was sitting inside me. I remember nothing more until I came around from the experience. My friend told me she'd had a lovely conversation with a gentleman. I was shocked. This was not part of the deal - I never agreed to do this at all, I was just helping a friend out. I told them never to do that again, under any circumstances, and to this day it hasn't. One evening we had the house rabbit out, when spirit came into the room. The rabbit started banging on the cage and I nearly leapt out of my chair. Lisa, who was listening, burst out laughing. I was glad she found it funny, but my heart nearly stopped. It was sad that the circle ceased after two years, but I knew there was a good reason and there's always a plan, so I just had to wait for the next episode.

I learned pretty quickly that the spirit world can manifest here on this plane of life. They can do it when we're in trouble, in pain and ill, suffering or about to pass over. I had seen them do it quite clearly when I was a child but I felt it was still the one hurdle I had to leap. Although I have seen and heard some amazing phenomena, it is a different thing to be able to convince others because it has to be unquestionable. Physical mediumship is not just working with the face, called transfiguration, but can also involve going into trance and speaking words. This can be seen as a lot more ambiguous. The medium enters a state where their own consciousness has moved aside and words of wisdom from the spirit world will flow through them for us to hear, either in their own voice or another.[3]

To work with the physical takes years of dedication and commitment. I know there are still physical circles up and down the country but they are apprehensive about bringing this out into the open as the

---

[3] This is how we have the teachings of White Eagle, which were brought through the wonderful medium Grace Cooke. White Eagle's teachings are truly beautiful and uplifting for the heart. As I understand it, he was a medium in the spirit world. Another physical medium was Estelle Roberts, who channelled Red Cloud, yielding one of my favourite books. There are many others who have created this phenomenon all over the world.

propensity for finger pointing and negativity is very great. Also, very strict rules of audience conduct are necessary in order to protect the medium from harm whilst they are in an altered state. Back in 2007, I started a physical circle in my home and we sat at the same time each week for about eighteen months, with some lovely phenomena of lights and noises. We experimented with different coloured light - blue, green, red and white, noting the different energy with each colour. When my brother Martin died, I was told by the spirit world to stop the circle, so I did; I was just told, "Not now, the time is not right." I always listen to them, because they know best.

This type of work is as much an experiment on the spirit side of life as it is on this side, and we have to work together and trust one another in order to create that miracle. There are three physical mediums I have seen who are excellent. One is David Thompson, who lives in Australia and visits the UK occasionally. I saw him at a very small place called Jenny's Sanctuary, where there is a room dedicated to physical mediumship named after the daughter of the gentleman who owns it. She is in spirit. David was truly amazing. A mixture of famous and other spirit people attended: Louis Armstrong seemed very authentic and Quentin Crisp was very amusing. As I understand from David, these voices have been verified by people who knew them. Spirit will use the energy in the room from the people and from the medium to create the magic of materialisations. What impressed me most on that evening was that he brought through the grandfather of a lady who was in the audience, who was completely unknown to him. He talked about her business and her family; it was excellent and detailed proof. All the people present had come from various places throughout the UK, and no-one knew anyone else. There are potential dangers for any medium working in this way. If certain rules of audience conduct are not observed it can severely harm the medium as they are working with elements and energies that we don't yet fully understand in this world. Look at it like fairy dust – it's something that can make the miracle happen, but it doesn't come from this world, it's just part of the recipe.

Anyone who knows nothing of this could think it sounds very far-fetched, but it's amazing and solid proof. If spirit could manage to bring physical phenomena out into the open, then it couldn't be denied any longer. Believe me, I know that there are many who are trying to achieve this on both sides of the veil. It's almost impossible to put into words how you feel when you hear or see something that defies all you know and believe, and all you've been taught.

A while ago we invited the transfiguration medium Jay Love to come to our church. We thought it would be good if people had the opportunity to experience this phenomenon, as it's quite rare. All my life, I never wanted physically to see anyone whom I knew was in the spirit world. I remembered how I'd felt all those years before when I'd seen my grandfather. But I was interested in what spirit could do and, if someone came through for someone else, I'd be happy, I could accept that. Then all week prior to the event I had an uneasy feeling. I asked spirit to keep away from me as there were many others who wanted and needed to experience it. There was also the fact that I was really scared my Dad might come through, because I just couldn't have coped with that. That would be my nemesis; I would crack and break. "No Daddy, I couldn't cope with that, please stay away."

Jay was rushed when he came in due to delays on the trains, so it was straight in to get changed and straight out again into the full room to start his evening. He gave a short talk in his broad Essex accent on what was expected, and what the spirit world expected of us, explaining that his voice would change. He is a lovely person and I liked him immediately. I sat on one side of him as he'd asked and closed my eyes while he talked. A beautiful peace descended on me and I smiled. Jay went quiet and when he spoke again the voice was totally different, a deeper, powerful and eloquent voice. It had the desired effect and caught everyone's attention. His guide started to impart a little information, and I was just relaxing and feeling the energies.

Then I became very aware of an energy that was very strong; I wanted to move away from it but I couldn't. The guide said he would like to speak to a Jacqui with 'links to number 6' (I lived at number 6) and 'links to Montrose' (I had just booked a group of readings in a Montrose Avenue). Everyone's eyes were upon me and I wanted to crawl away and hide. I really didn't want to do this. Mum broke the silence by making noises towards me so I knew I had to. I got up from my chair and moved to the seat in front of him. He took my hands, his eyes closed as he leaned forward slightly and smiled. His guide said, "You were dreading this weren't you?" They knew – they'd heard my pleas and yet still they came. I sat rooted to the chair, begging my Dad not to come forward…

The room was silent. When he spoke again he started to talk about my Dad, who'd been with me all my life. I shook my head but he nodded. He asked me if I could remember my Dad's eyes. Of course I could, they were the bluest eyes ever! He said, "Watch." I gazed into his eyes and they changed colour! I was shocked, and the feeling overwhelmed me as the tears took hold. Oh God, not here, not now. Then he said, "There is another here tonight who knew this gentleman." Indeed there was. Mum came up and sat with me. He came forward again and she inhaled sharply with shock - she could see him too. "Look Jac," she said, "he's here!" I closed my eyes tighter but Mum was talking now, about how she could see his thick eyebrows and his beautiful eyes. She was stunned. Others could see it too but I craved for the ground to swallow me up. This was just too close for comfort. The guide then turned to me and said, "You have a beautiful Chinese guide. Do you know what he looks like?" I said I did, and he replied, "Watch." The moustache grew very long, and I saw it clearly.

When you see something like this it cements your belief quite strongly. It shakes you up and you really can't deny the facts there in front of you. To be fair to everyone, some people didn't see anything. But if you don't open your hearts and your minds, then you won't. You have to play your part. Some people never will see. The physical phenomenon is made from ectoplasm, a 'stuff' made within the medium that looks white and wispy, a bit like muslin. Physical mediumship very much depends on audience energy for its creation. The energy in the room is paramount. So if you attend such a session, send it from your hearts and amazing proof can come to this world. The spirit world need a hand to bring the physical manifestations, they can't do it on their own yet.

The next day Jay was doing some readings and I had booked one, which is unusual for me. I hadn't had a reading in many years, but I thought it might be fun. When I walked into the room, Jay looked at me very seriously which didn't seem like him as he'd been full of mischief all day. He told me that this reading was not going to be like others I'd received as he had some information from the spirit world that I needed to hear. He told me that my Dad had been with me every day of my life and that I'd never been alone. I listened quietly. He gave me very accurate information about my brothers in spirit and about my Dad and my spirit friends.

Then he told me that I was writing a book and that I had to finish it. I scoffed at this point. I mean, who would want to read a book about me? It was pointed out to me that the book was not just about me, but is also for all of you who may have gone through similar tragedies and painful episodes in your lives. You need to know that you are never alone, and to know that you can get through to 'the other side' because I have, so you can too. I just found it amazing that anyone would want to hear about my experiences but I was told that people all over the world go through something similar, and some have no way of finding help in dealing with it - this book would guide them. When he finished the reading, I was very pensive. I had only tentatively written a few thousand words and I'm no writer. Was I really to finish this work? How and what was I supposed to write about? I went to spirit and they told me to share what I could as a start, and when I'd done that they would tell me a little more. So I wrote more and more, until the truth was laid bare, more than I intended to share originally. I have been called brave to include it, but if it helps someone then the journey was worth it.

Many people may find all this scary. Is it real? Only you can tell. Only you can follow what your soul needs to know, so don't be narrow-minded, feel the fear and do it anyway. The proof of spirit's existence is there to be found.

We've had some wonderful mediums in the past, Helen Duncan being the most famous. She was the last person to be arrested under the Witchcraft Act of 1735. She was tried at the Old Bailey in 1944 because she brought through a son, who had died in action during the war, to his mother before anyone else knew of his demise, including the government. She was a rare talent and very special, but was never exonerated or pardoned and to this day there are people who fight to clear her name. It was a terrible miscarriage of justice and the label 'witch' should be expunged. She was no more a witch than I am.

Leslie Flint was another direct voice medium, and there was also John Sloan who sat with Arthur Findlay. Arthur's interest and dedication was such that he left his home to the Spiritualist National Union to advance the cause of spiritual communication and teaching. I am always one for proof that is tangible and can be passed on to the world. If you research mediumship, you will find a great number of tests and scientific studies have been done all over the world through the years, and some of the evidence is hard to ignore. That said, you have to make up your own mind. Has the spirit world managed to convince you?

CHAPTER THIRTEEN

Healing

*God, however you perceive Him, used energy and created
all living things and it is as it is, so nothing can be
added and nothing taken away; we should feel
blessed and in awe of that miracle.*

Healing was never something I really thought about. Looking back, I suppose I had been doing it for many years, with Graham, Ernie and the hundreds of people I have helped. I would always be on call, always there for people who needed me. That was what I was here for and I have never thought any different. It was just part of being me.

I was with my brother Graham as he lay sleeping in hospital and I was massaging his feet, when a gentleman came walking towards me. He was dressed all in black with a Stetson hat and spurs, looking very menacing, as if he'd stepped off the set of a Wild West film. He had dark, ominous eyes and stood very still, just watching me. Then suddenly, out of thin air, he grabbed a white doctor's coat and put it on, smiled and nodded at me, and vanished. As you can imagine, I could not believe my eyes. I shook my head and looked around to see if anyone else had seen him. Obviously no-one had. Then that night I was in bed and I saw him again, looking quite solid. As I peeped from under the covers, very scared, his eyes wrinkled slightly as if he were going to smile and he told me directly that he'd come to help me with my healing. He was American, and in his younger years he'd been a gunfighter; but he'd turned away from that and become an apothecary. I was to call him Ben. I told him that I didn't do healing, but he just smiled and told me that I would soon. Then he vanished as quickly as he'd come.

When I completed my reflexology course, I volunteered to work at the local hospice. To me that was just a joy because the healing helps on deeper levels, bringing relaxation and pain relief just when and where people need it. The hospice was a beautiful place overlooking luscious green gardens with a tree you just wanted to hug all the time - it had a remarkable energy. At the time I didn't know much about energy; I always felt something but I didn't have a clue what it was. There was a team of volunteers working with the patients who gave their time freely with many alternative therapies, which the patients loved. This service was provided steadily and to this day is a valued part of the hospice's work.

A while later I was contacted about a healing course that the hospice was providing on site. It would be done over two years, with different levels, and I was told in no uncertain terms by spirit that I should be doing this. I didn't want to, as by this time I was so busy with my other spirit work that I just didn't know how I was going to fit everything in. But somehow I did. The course was accredited and could be used all over the country. Nowadays, spiritual healing is available in some hospitals.

Spiritual energy, as I see it, is the continuous life force. It is what continues after the physical body has passed. But it is also part of the life force that is in all of us, in everything that lives on this planet. In other cultures it is called 'chi' or 'prana'. There is also electrical energy, thicker and denser, and used in the physical body. The etheric or spirit energy can be directed through the mind and by intention can be sent anywhere it is needed, via the heart centre of the physical body. This thought power is huge and has unlimited potential. It can be tapped into by every living person. If used by enough people with love, it could transform society as we know it. It is heart-powered unconditional love which can be sent anywhere, at any time, by anyone. When are we all going to understand this?

Try focusing your energy on a situation and asking for help. Then get out the way and allow the work to be done - energy always has a way to find its goal. Healing can be sent by thought for body, mind or spirit, and it is your intention that counts. Where do you want it to go? Why do you want to send it? What do you want it to do? This all links together to make that wave of love go exactly where it needs to be, always to the right place at the right time. You can ask in your mind, out loud or silently, it doesn't make any difference; prayer is prayer, and prayer is thought no matter what you call it. I like to see it as a rope. Each of us sends out a tendril to make it thicker and stronger, then that rope becomes the rope of hope and it will do its work. It knows its purpose.

Healing does not always do what we hope for. For example, if a person is going to pass over to the spirit world then they will, although the healing will do much to ease that passing. It is always our choice of when to pass from this world to the next. Why is that? Well, we choose our lives here, every bit of them. I have been told this direct by spirit. (They tell me that we choose to come back sometimes into the same family, not to pick and choose the good or not so good experiences, but because that's what we need to move forward.) I loved giving healing. But I would get called to the hospital, or go and visit someone, and the next day they passed to spirit. In one year this happened three times and I started to get a bit worried! But they were going to pass anyway, and I've been told many times that the healing helped them to let go and be at peace quickly in the spirit world. Many people are afraid of death, afraid of letting go. But the fact is that death is part of physical life, it's the final phase, the energy shift that moves us back to the spiritual form that we originally were.

I frequently get asked, "How do I heal? How do I share? How do I give? Why am I here? What should I be doing?" Well, you don't have to look far; the answers are inside you. The way to start your quest is to find a quiet place. Given today's lifestyles, quiet places can be hard to find. There is too much to do in the day, and we continue to hold on to busy thoughts too long. Let them go and the answer will magically appear. The more earnestly you look, the more you block it. Then there are often signs to watch out for too, synchronicities that may appear around you again and again. Notice them. Think about what you truly want.

Ian was someone I'd been healing for only a few weeks; he was very poorly with bowel cancer, but the loveliest of men and quite young too. His partner, Julie, had invited me over to see if I could help him. I gave the healing and he loved it, then he started to talk to me about strange experiences he had gone through. He was a very spiritual man, certainly not perfect, but those who knew him loved him dearly and I became very fond of him in the short time I knew him.

One evening I went to a committee meeting at the local Spiritualist church, where I was Secretary at the time. I was going to do some healing after the meeting, as I did every week on the same night, but during the evening I heard a voice clearly and audibly say, "Go and see Ian now!" I stood up and told everyone I had to go - it's a good job they all knew me. I ran out of the church and drove as fast as my little car would go across town, arrived and knocked on the door. Julie answered it and said that Ian had drawn his last breath and died just seconds before. He was on a bed in the lounge and as I walked in I saw that his mum was in the room too. I walked over to the bed and said a silent prayer for him. It was a sad moment.

Julie asked me if I would still give him healing. Well, I'd never given healing for a recently departed soul before, but if that's what she wanted then that's what she would get. She told me, "He was waiting for you." I felt very humbled. As I started the healing, making my way around the bed, it was strange to feel that his energy was still there, but different. Then I was suddenly aware of Ian standing beside me and talking to me, very matter-of-factly. I told him silently that I couldn't communicate there and then and that he should wait, but he was very insistent. When I'd finished, I turned to Julie and thanked her. Then Ian started to talk to me again, about someone who he didn't want to miss the funeral. I asked Julie, as gently as I could, if she minded me talking to her. She agreed. I told her what Ian had said and the person turned out to be his best friend from where he used to live in the south. He talked a little more and then thanked me for helping with his transition. I didn't know what to say - he just smiled and left. I often wonder who taught whom that night. Ian gave me a great gift, an experience that has never left me. It was like I was meant to be there, but for a higher reason. For all the souls involved in that, I thank you.

There were times afterwards when he would come back to Julie and make noises. He would move things and it scared her, as it scares most people. Please be aware that they don't do it to scare you, but because they love you. I still send healing to Julie; she is someone I watch over and help whenever she needs it.

The energy of light and its colours has a healing quality. We may sometimes feel a need to wear or wrap a colour around us. Try using that colour when you wake up in the morning. Listen to what your body is telling you and feel the effects that different colours have on you. Don't just wear that black jumper because it's nearest or the only thing that doesn't need ironing; wear something stronger and you'll feel very different in it. We've all seen businessmen who wear grey suits and muted colours; how would it be if someone turned up in a brightly coloured suit? Why not? Just because tradition dictates what should be worn, doesn't mean it can't be done. You should see some of the colourful dresses I wear when I'm working… I always get compliments and people say, "What a lovely dress, but I couldn't wear it, it's not for me." Why is it not for you?

Trust your instincts and wear the colours that feel right for you; they will also help to strengthen your chakras. These are the energy centres in the body's field, and the seven main chakras are aligned along the spinal column. The word is Sanskrit for 'wheel', and as this suggests they are spinning vortices. There are chakras connected to every organ, gland and body system and each is related to a particular colour's vibration. If there are disturbances at any level, this shows in the chakra's vitality level. Also, each chakra has intelligence, which means that they are not only associated with our physical health, but also aspects of our emotional and psychological systems.

The energy field around the body is called the aura and it contains information about its host. It shows the true nature of our moods and intentions - we can't hide anything there. Some people can see the aura quite easily, and children often find it easier to see as they are closer to the spirit world. The aura is basically egg-shaped. Our hands are particularly sensitive to energy in the aura, and indeed I can always feel it when I am giving healing to someone else. When I have healing myself, I find it painful for anyone to put their hands above my head because it feels like someone is pressing down on me. Many people have seen and felt my aura, and I am told it is quite large. I believe it may be affected by the strength of the spiritual connection one has.

We need to learn how to protect our own energy, as there are people who will drain it from us. I'm sure we have all come across people whose company leaves us exhausted after a while, and after they've gone we feel like we've run a marathon. Something I learned is that we can limit our energy being drained if we 'cross our circuits', so to speak. It may sound a strange thing to say, but I found it works: cross your legs, your arms, your fingers, and put yourself in a protective bubble in your mind's eye. This will limit the energy that others can take from you.

The pineal gland is about the size of a pea and lies behind the nose and eyes. It is activated by light and works in harmony with the hypothalamus. Among spiritual people it is known as the connecting link between the spiritual and the physical worlds, and is also called 'the third eye'. The development of psychic talents is closely associated with this gland, so practise focussing on the third eye to become more familiar with spiritual energy. Indeed I have tried this many times in my teaching, using a mandala wheel, to see auras. We should use all the colours in this world to strengthen our awareness of energy at all the different levels, spiritual, physical and emotional.

CHAPTER FOURTEEN

Some Help and Understanding

You know you can't make wrong decisions, just decisions.
When you believe in yourself, you will have the truth and the
trust that is right for you. Any decision you make leads to
growth of your spirit and to new levels of understanding.

What happens when we die and go to the spirit world? Many people have written about that in very detailed and eloquent ways, and I don't know what else I can say to convince people of its existence. If one doesn't want to believe, one never will (until one sees things as they really are), but I've had many new communicators from the spirit world who have been very surprised to find they are still very much alive when they cross over! Everyone here has a perspective on the subject. My husband doesn't believe in any afterlife, but that's his prerogative (and if I go first, I'll be waiting there to say "I told you so!"). I can't change his mind, it's up to him. But here's the thing, some people don't want to know and I have to respect that and only work where there are like-minded people. I don't wish to offend anyone.

Working for the spirit world every day is a joy and I would love to give this proof to all, even those who don't want to know, because when you 'go over' it can be difficult to adjust. I am told that this is different for every soul, and one can take all the time one needs. When this is done, we have choices of what we want to do and whether to go off on our own or follow the happy throng. Where do you fit in? Do you even want to?

There is work for all who want it. My brother Graham chose to assist people who pass over quickly in war, disaster or through an accident. This was entirely his choice and I know he's very busy. (I'm not sure what that says about this world.) My brother Martin doesn't work with him, but chooses to work with people who take their own lives. It is always about education and love, and you can be with whom you are meant to be with. Your spirit will know where it has to go. There is always help for everyone who needs it, and I know that I am helped every step of the way. I am sometimes hurt deeply by people who are rude and confrontational, but I do what I've been put here for and I am supported. Many in the spirit world choose to come back and work with us. You may have people around you who knew you, but the majority will be people you haven't known. They may even stretch back through time and have been someone famous. Well, why not? After all, they were only famous on this side of life and everyone is equal on the other side. Spirit always comes to us in forms that we can prove and recognise, so when they return through a medium it is as they were when they were here. They are remembering their physical existence.

Let me tell you about some of my 'spirit team', those who work with me or at least the ones I know about. I have explained about Ben, who comes to assist in my healing work. I also have the Chinese gentleman who has been with me as long as I can remember - he always brings me news, good or otherwise – and even when I first started my visualisations I would see him clearly. "But how do you know he's real?" I hear you ask. Well, all I can say is that I just 'know'. I have seen him and felt his presence. I used to wonder why I have a love of the orient, with several oriental figures in my home including one that looks just like him.

One day I was working at my desk, absorbed in a completely different thought process, when I was aware of this Chinese man standing next to me (I always know when there is someone with me) and we had a conversation that went something like this:

"Hello. Who are you?"

"Someone who has been with you a long time."

"Oh, ok, do I know you?"

"Yes, you have seen me in your thoughts."

"Ok then, tell me your name."

"Mmm … you can call me Fah Hian."

Now, I talk to spirit people as I would to anyone here on Earth. They know I have complete respect for them, but I like to be in control; I find it hard to relinquish that. But this voice was clear and precise; he even spelled the name out for me. Despite knowing what I do, I still have doubts. After all, I'm imperfect. I didn't believe for one minute that I would find out any more about this, but still I jotted it down on a piece of paper and went back to my work. The visit was very brief and I didn't think too much of it because I am used to people around me most of the time. I then forgot about it until I got home. That evening, after supper, I decided to check it out just to see what I could find, and discovered that Fah Hian was a fourth century Chinese missionary who went to India with Sung Yun. The fact that he existed at all was a shock. Fah Hian now works alongside my energy, bringing beautiful words and teachings. I am not at all learned but I find I know just the words to speak with him near me. He is very special to me. That's all I need to know, and there's no need to complicate matters.

Mr Hat Man is someone whose Earthly identity I don't know, although he is a powerful part of the group. He dresses in a long black coat and a tall black hat. He first appeared to me about six months before Ernie died. I was sitting at the back of the church when this man walked through the door from the kitchen and strode confidently down towards me. I froze. He looked real, very solid and imposingly scary, and it was obvious that no-one else could see him. He had dark eyes, a pointed face and a small pointy beard. My heart raced as I turned my head to stare directly into his eyes. Then he bowed low and faded out as quickly as he had appeared. I had to get out, so I slipped outside and called a friend. I needed to hear a friendly voice of reassurance. She laughed, chastising me for my reaction after all the other things I had experienced.

It always scares the heck out of me when they appear to me like this. The experience was hard to let go of for a while as he'd had quite an impact, but I said nothing and put it to the back of my mind along with the rest. The next Friday was circle which I couldn't go to, but the follow-ing week my friend who had attended walked in holding an A3 piece of paper. She told me that someone from the circle had contacted her. She'd drawn a man she had seen in the church, walking around the circle as if looking for something. She felt compelled to give it to my friend, but she knew it was for me: a drawing of a slim man dressed in a black coat with a tall hat. My breath caught in my throat when I saw it - the likeness was amazing. He still comes to me occasionally, issues his instructions and is very brusque. There are never any arguments from me! I don't know who he was or what he did. He won't tell me. I suppose they don't have to if they don't want to - sometimes they can be very human.

My main man is beautiful. He is someone I have worked with a great deal and some people have seen him with me as I give out mes-sages. He's a Red Indian gentleman, and a gentle man. We work very well together. He is patient, loving and understanding, he laughs at me and sometimes shakes his head in despair, but he still comes back time after time. Sometimes I see him older with a feather headdress, and I also see him younger. He is playful and likes to laugh with me, but when we work together he is serious. But then my work is very serious to me. This is people's lives I am dealing with.

Now I move on to Queen Victoria. I understand now that I saw this lady previously in my 'dream' when I was ill in hospital, but didn't connect her to that at first. She took quite a while to come back to me, but when she did it was in a development circle at the beginning of my teaching path. Someone showed me a picture of a lady, with a hat and feather in it, which they had seen in the room whilst the circle was going on. They felt compelled to look further, eventually identifying the picture, and I recognised her as the lady I had seen previously. It was Queen Victoria. That still makes me chuckle as I've always had a great interest in and passion for this woman. She was very beautiful and passionate, and small like me. We have a lot in common! A while later, I was told that the old Spiritualist church in the town used to be in Queen Street, and Victoria would come to Leamington Spa to take the waters, and would visit the church to try to contact her Albert. I have never been able to verify this as I'm sure she wouldn't have made it public. She still comes to visit from time to time, seems to know when I need her and really does help me.

Every year in November, a representative of the Spiritualist church is invited to lay a wreath for the fallen with the Mayor's party and our church officers always attend. The treasurer Annie and I arrived at one such event on a cold November morning. I stepped into the Town Hall through the large double doors of the very grand building, which has an effigy of Queen Victoria standing proudly in front of it. I had never been in there before. There stood Victoria in all her finery. I smiled at her and she walked up the beautiful staircase. I turned to Annie and told her that Queen Victoria was on the stairs. She looked at me very bemused and I just smiled. We attended the wreath laying, hurried back to the Town Hall to get warm, and walked upstairs and along the corridor to the main hall. We collected a drink and sat down for a few minutes before leaving.

A lovely lady came to sit at our table. I didn't know her, but Annie did and they were talking together. Then the lady turned to me and asked if I had seen the mayoral chambers. "Er, no!" I said. So she reached for my hand and said, "Come with me." I looked at Annie and she just urged me on, not sure what this was all about. Just outside the room she released my hand and I followed her down a corridor until we came to a beautifully polished, heavy wooden door. With effort she pushed it open and inside was a beautiful room with items from all over the world. I didn't really know why I was there but dutifully walked around the room trying to look interested. She was standing on the other side of the room, in front of a beautiful parchment. As she lifted it, I froze and immediately understood the connection. I knew who had arranged this! There was the Royal Warrant to make Leamington Spa 'Royal'. There was Victoria's name and her seal. I was stunned. I don't know how many people get to see that, but I knew I was seeing something very special and I felt humble. It was a very surreal moment and a privilege. I knew Victoria was there with me that day. I knew she was around me, as she always does seem to be on official occasions.

Why me? I don't have a clue. You would have to ask her that. The spirit world is always telling me that I am worthy of all I receive. All of us are worthy of our small miracles. We are all entitled to know that we are not alone. So look for the signs from your family and friends, who are always around you; sometimes they are so obvious you just can't see them for the life of you. Talk to your helpers, to your spirit friends; we all have them. Notice your thoughts. Ask for what you would like then see what happens.

When I started attending the Spiritualist church way back, I met a gentleman called David Cheyne. He was, and still is, very much loved. He was drawn to the church because he had lost his son in a motorbike accident; it brought him the solace he needed and, eventually, the proof that his son was just fine. He had no spiritual gifts that he was aware of when he began to attend the church, but through attending circles he did develop an amazing gift. He became a psychic artist. This means he could draw and paint with direct assistance from the spirit world (though he couldn't actually draw or paint before he came to the church). He described it as 'someone leading his hand' to create the amazing pictures and faces. He was also a musician and would play the guitar. He loved music and was very well known in the Spiritualist churches in the UK.

Everyone who met him loved him. He just couldn't stop talking about spirit; in fact he couldn't stop talking at all! I loved his infectious nature and he always made me laugh, though sometimes he frustrated me because I could never get anything done when he was around. David was very helpful to me over the years and I owe him such gratitude. He would walk into the church and have a hug and a word for everyone. He would hug me and whisper in my ear, "You're my favourite" and kiss my cheek. It made me smile, and it became a bit of a saying between us. Then David passed to spirit very suddenly. Every Sunday he went swimming and then went to the park for a while. This particular day as he sat on a bench he had a heart attack. It was a sad day and he is still very much missed by all who knew him; the spirit world gained a true angel that day.

In 2008 David painted a picture for my birthday. I was at the church and he came bounding over to me, wishing me a happy birthday and said that spirit had told him to paint a picture for me. His enthusiasm was as infectious as ever. It was a beautiful picture with two pathways on it. There was a huge angel at the end of one path, and a face, clearly that of a Chinese gentleman. It meant so much to me and I felt humble that he had painted it for me, as his paintings were always in demand. I took it home that evening and placed it on the wall next to the bed so that I could look at it every night. It would be the last thing I saw before I closed my eyes and one of the first things I saw in the morning. What better way to sleep and wake than with an angel watching over me?

I studied the picture very hard over the years and I knew every detail. It was the angel watching over me that meant so much. It was not long before the picture started to move, to one side and then to the other. Each morning I would straighten it, and overnight it would move again. That made me smile. Then a miracle happened... I didn't believe it myself initially. Now, I do know how this sounds, it seems impossible but it happened. This picture had been in the same place for nearly four years and I would gaze at it before I closed my eyes at night, saying a prayer for whoever needed it, sending healing for everyone. This one night I was gazing absentmindedly at it on the wall when I became aware that someone was in the room with me. They prodded me. I asked, "What?" They said, "Look at the picture." I was getting a bit frustrated. "What about the picture?" Then as I stared at it, something started to register; so I took it off the wall and studied it closely. As the realisation set in, my jaw dropped in astonishment.

The picture had changed. It was painted in oils straight onto a small canvas, not framed and still in its raw state. But the angel was now clearer – before, she just had a gold blob for her head, but now she had two eyes, a nose and a mouth, added in a rather childlike manner. One path in the picture had been very rocky, but now the rocks had gone and the pathway was smooth. The major change was the head of the Chinese man, which was further up the picture than it had been originally. Everything seemed elevated, clearer and more succinct. There were also two rabbits that had been added in gold pen, within the trunk of the tree. It took quite a while for all this to sink in and for me to be able to discuss it with anyone. I am lucky. People who know me believed me. I do know how unbelievable this sounds, but it happened.

2012 was a poignant year in many ways for many people. It marked a spiritual revolution and a spiritual awakening, a time to understand who we really are and what we are really capable of doing as we go forward. I never expected myself to be part of this awakening. But recently, a small inner goddess has raised her head over the parapet and is ready for action. What that is, I don't know. I'm just waiting for spirit to let me in on that crucial piece of information.

CHAPTER FIFTEEN

You Want More?

We are in fact spirit having a human experience.
When we are scared to try new experiences, it is only
fear that we have created ourselves because we
do not know what the outcome will be.

'More' is a very provocative word, I think. It can bring so much promise.
I would like more too - more for others though, not for myself. Yes, I
want to be able to earn enough to support my family and to drive a red
Audi convertible while I'm doing it. That would be very nice, but there's
no guarantee I'm going to do either. If it is to happen, it will at the time it
is meant to and not before. Things always come they are meant to, no
matter what we do. How frustrating is that? Why do we have to wait?
Yet sometimes waiting a little longer will bring the ideal solution and
make your dreams come true. How often do the words 'trust' and
'patience' come out in readings? Are you satisfied with your lot? We may
tell ourselves that we are happy and content, but is that true?

Are you rich or poor? The poor always feel that others have more
but we can be rich in many ways, with our family, our friends and our
pets. What is it that makes us feel special and brings us joy? I feel that I,
like everyone else, am rich with knowledge. I can walk through each
day of my life knowing that I can bring much love to people on this side
of life from their loved ones. I know that I am never alone, and that
everything I do has a purpose whether or not I know what it is. I meet a

great number of people who feel isolated, lost, ostracised and lonely. I want to fix the world and I know I can't, but that doesn't stop me trying. I use my energy and ask my helpers to assist others no matter where they are in the world. People tell me I am special to do what I do but I am not special, I am just me and this is my job. I try to make people feel loved and special because they need that, and when no-one around them can ease their soul, spirit always can.

Every one of us is rich in many ways and there is much that we can give. We should care as much as we can about each other, and help as much as we are able to. That's what we used to do before modern society started to distract us. Progress is good but not when basic human values are forgotten. In times of great upheaval in the world we seem to be able to pull together, so why can't we do that in everyday life? Something is very wrong when people turn away from the perse-cuted peoples of this world, just because we can. Is it all right to see people starving, when we have more than enough to eat? Is it that way because we have more freedom, more choices? Shouldn't every indi-vidual be entitled to make a choice to have more?

There are many who do understand the true beauty of this world we live in, and want to look after it, cherish it, enabling all the life forms she sustains to live a peaceful existence. She has such a beautiful energy yet we treat her badly. We think we need more and we take it from her; so what happens when that is all gone?

The spirit world knows all, sees all and hears all. They know that it's difficult for us to experience pain in this life, but in the end it brings clarity, as it never goes on forever. Eventually peace and beauty can come to us, when we choose to listen to the quiet inner mind where the real part of us lives. Let each of us, in our own unique lives, use the spirit as our guide every day. We must believe in and trust ourselves too. When we are in pain, we just need to ask the spirit world for help and it will be given. There is no need to stay in that relationship that scares us, or that job that we can't abide, or that house that doesn't feel right. We must take the chance that there is always more out there for us - if we would only look and believe in the possibility that change is possible. There is always a solution.

The power of God, however you perceive Him (or Her or It), does indeed move in mysterious ways. We are in fact spirit having a human experience. When we are scared to try new experiences, it is only fear that we have created ourselves because we do not know what the outcome will be. That's a very human reaction and completely normal. But imagine how good it would be to at least give change a try. Sometimes we just have to live all we can, try as many experiences as we can and strive to be the best that we can be, no matter who holds us back (usually ourselves). Our capacity to develop our personal power is endless.

I believe that we choose our Earth pathway before we arrive here; we then live it in accordance with our own rules. Everything we need to know is programmed into us at a deep unconscious level, there to be accessed when we need it. We are each travelling along our own life's journey, remembering what we need to experience and when. This creates our memories and our feelings, and defines who we are. However you see your God - whether it is a deity or an energy - is entirely personal. Look at it this way - there are many doors which all lead to the one divine place.

Now you may not agree with that description. But I would not judge anyone for their beliefs, because I consider all people to be of no less value than me. So I ask others to respect my beliefs and consider them. In the past, when I've mentioned that I'm a Spiritualist, I've had some horrified looks, been ignored and given the cold shoulder, and been accused of being in league with the devil and putting my immortal soul in danger! Do I care when people say such things? From a personal perspective, not really, but it makes me very sad when others do not try to understand. For that approach holds us back; we cannot see more if we are blinkered. After all, seeking divine help or saying a prayer, in some form, is something that we all do at times. Some people tell me that they don't because it's 'embarrassing', yet asking 'God help me' is just a figure of speech… or is it?

What's important is that we try to look for the good in our lives, even if it's only a seed. We must put one foot in front of the other and take one step at a time, love and respect ourselves then go out into the world and give others the same love and respect. I'm not saying it's easy, but it's so worthwhile. Adopting the universal language of "I care" can make such a difference in the lives of others, when we try and spread love and assistance. Someday we may need it in return! And the more we give, the more we will receive.

At some point in all of our lives we feel that something needs to change, somehow we need to move on but we may not have a clue how to do it. It's at a time like this that people need to pay most attention to what is going on around them.

For me it was the death of my brother Graham which was the turning point. Many people find their way to a spiritual place following the loss of a loved one, or following a major upheaval in their lives. Whatever it is that brings us to such a place, we shall find nothing but love. I had absolutely no comprehension of what was to come when I first stepped into a Spiritualist church. I could not foresee how this visit was going to make me revisit all I had lived through, but in a new and brighter light which would take over my life in a wonderful way.

Then when I started to be able to give clairvoyance, there were some lovely messages for the audience and I was very interested in their reactions. I love to watch people, you can learn so much about them (and most of the time it is not what they say but what they don't). When I realised what I could do, I wanted to tell everyone... But guess what? Not everyone wanted to know. This was a bit of a shock for me because I didn't realise that some people would feel so strongly about talking to their loved ones in spirit. I couldn't understand why that would be a problem for them. It was a learning experience for me – some people really didn't want to know (and some were very rude). I learned the hard way that there's a time and a place. Now I know that I will be where I am needed, and whoever needs to see me will be brought to me.

Every spirit worker in this world has their own way of working, and no two are the same. But we are all working for the same boss - be very sure of that! To work for spirit can be tough and exhausting, yet so fulfilling. It can bring such clarity to our existence. The commitment and the love connection are made between us and our spirit friends every day. They are spirit and we are spirit. We are all one. For many years now I have been working hard for the spirit world and it's a joy for me, remembering what I need at just the right time for each place and bringing some amazing evidence to people all over the country. I have spoken to people from every walk of life, from every social group and of every age; they all leave amazed and uplifted, but then so do I.

I have stopped all my fighting with 'them'. I remember it being a conscious decision. I threw my hands up in resignation and just accepted whatever spirit brought to me. That acceptance made everything so much clearer. Why was I so obstinate, and for so long? Eventually, I learned to look at each experience for its merits, not its negativities. After all, everything just is as it is. We don't have to fight everything and everyone. We can just accept ourselves for who we have to be.

After my reading with Jay Love (see Chapter 12) my life simply changed. I went to work as usual. I was tired, but it was more than a physical tiredness, it was frustration and irritation, something that I couldn't quite identify. All day there were tears and I couldn't have stopped them if I'd tried. I felt as if there were a huge hole within me. I felt bereft, grieving, but I didn't know what for.

After work the next day, the hole was growing and I had no idea what to do. I wanted my Dad so badly, so I decided to go to his grave. I hadn't done this for many years, but felt a deep compulsion to go. The evening was lovely, warm and sunny, and the aromas of the trees wrapped themselves around me as I walked down the path towards the grave. I was glad that it was at the back of the churchyard where I could hide. I couldn't explain how I felt to anyone, so I knew I had to reach out further.

I reached the grave and noticed that someone had recently cut the grass. When I studied the gravestone I saw that it was very faded now and I couldn't see too many of the words, though 'husband' and 'father' were clearly readable. There were no flowers on the grave because Mum had been ill that week. I didn't think he would mind. Tears filled my eyes. I wanted to be with him so badly and felt his loss acutely. I was coming up to forty-nine years of age and I noted that he was forty-nine when he died. I wanted him to hold me and tell me I was going to get over this. I'd thought I was a strong person and I knew I had learned much, but I felt small and insignificant, desolate and lost. I lay down on the grave as I did when I was a child, curling my legs up in a foetal position. I said, "Daddy, I need to be with you."

I needed him, and he came. Within the blink of an eye I was in a garden attached to beautiful house, and I recognised it from being shown it many times by spirit. It was the house of my paternal grandparents, which had been demolished many years ago. I used to come here a lot in my dreams. A couple of times before, I've been 'transported' to another place in time and space, as if there are worlds within worlds.

From the house, the way into the garden was down five steps with a lion on a plinth at the base of the steps. In front was a beautiful rose garden, full of colour and in full bloom. As I walked past that, there was an expanse of grass and, in the corner, an overhanging tree. Attached between two trees was a swinging bench, out of the sun; you could almost believe it to be a fairy arbour with the trees making a circular shape around it. It was deep green with layers of leaves on the ground, spongy as I walked on it. On reaching the arbour, I ducked slightly and peered inside; it was much darker and cooler in the shade. I smiled as I recognised this place. I had always been here alone; no-one ever came with me. It was comfortable and safe and I could hide here for a while.

I sat down on the bench. It swung slightly and I was able to reach the ground. Looking around, not much had changed since I'd visited before, as if time had stood still. But then there is no time in the spirit world, so it would, I suppose. I thought, "Am I in the spirit world? Or somewhere inbetween? Or am I somewhere else entirely?" Each time had been different, but this time it was personal - I wanted to be here and I didn't want to go back.

I was hoping that my Dad might appear. I'd never asked him to before - to see him would have broken me, so I was resigned that he wouldn't come to me. After all, I knew that you couldn't 'summon' anyone to come from the spirit world. But then I saw him. He rippled into view at the edge of the house and just stared in my direction. My heart raced, I wanted to run to him but I was frozen. He started to walk across the grass from the house and I just watched him… it was the way he'd always walked, the way he'd swung his arms. He stood at the entrance to the arbour, stared at me for a few seconds and smiled. He was just how I remembered him, his eyes so blue. He ducked slightly to enter the arbour, very slowly walked over to where I sat and stood in front of me. We studied each other, then I slowly stood up and he wrapped his arms around me, holding me close. I lowered my head onto his shoulder and sobbed, my body shaking with pain and pleasure; I let it flow and he didn't stop me. When it eased I pulled away from him and he released me, but still held my hand. We sat down and faced each other. He smiled - it was still crooked. I have the same smile, too many lips and not enough teeth.

How do you start a conversation like this? So much had happened, so much life had gone past, and I was not the child I had been.

"I have always been with you, Jacqueline. From the day I left, I have seen everything." I swallowed hard at that; he seemed to read my mind, chuckled and shook his head. "Don't worry about any of it, you've always gone your own way and lived how you chose. Much of it was painful," he added thoughtfully.

"You need to know," he continued, "why you feel so empty now. It's because you have released the block that you had regarding me. It was such a heavy weight in your heart, and it became part of who you are. Jacqui, you stopped yourself knowing my presence - I was here but you refused to believe. You never have believed your own worthiness. I am so very proud of you. I love you, and you'll see how worthy you are in times to come."

I sat transfixed and very still. I didn't want to come out of this too soon. In fact, I don't think I wanted to come out of it at all. He was here, and we were together.

"Daddy, I don't know how to fill it. I don't know what to do next. I don't like this feeling, I feel like a child, so scared." He stared at me, incredulous.

"You are a child. My child." That caught me right in the heart. "Fill it with life now. *Live.* Don't be scared. Say no. Say yes. Do something - but do it for you. Cherish yourself as you should, you're still on the Earth, and that's how it should be. You have a lot of work to do. Everything is exactly is as it is meant to be."

I touched his arm - he felt solid – and he smiled, hugging me close. I wanted to talk to him for hours, to tell him everything, but I knew he already knew. There was no need for words now, and I could sense that this time with him was coming to an end. I wished I could have quelled that rising panic. I didn't want to go back alone. He knew, and as he stood and held me at arm's length he looked as emotional as I was.

"Remember Jacqueline, you are my greatest achievement. I love you." I couldn't speak, so just mouthed, "I love you too." He smiled and started to fade, melting away in front of my eyes. I felt the tears falling down my face and I fell to my knees and curled up on the ground. Then as quickly as I'd left, I was back in the churchyard and awoke with a start, with tears staining my cheeks.

I sat up and hugged my knees, wiping my face on my arm and trying to make sense of what I'd just experienced. Was it my imagination? I was suddenly reminded that I knew better than that when both my Indian and Chinese angels appeared by my side. They were there to remind me that I was not alone. I breathed deeply. How did I feel? Lighter, much lighter. A little sore in my heart but, yes, I did feel better. I turned my face to the gravestone and said, "Thanks Daddy."

How long had I been here? It only seemed like a few minutes but it had been about half an hour. As I turned to walk away, I could still hear his voice and recall his features. I realised how lucky I was, and that here and now was the next big shift; the one person whom I thought had left me when I needed him most, and who had started me on this pathway, had been there every day of my life. I needed to let that sink in.

Walking back up the pathway, I turned and looked back at the gravestone. There was a holly tree growing behind it that had been there since I was a child. It had just rooted itself, deciding where it wanted to be. It was strong and green and proud, and close to my father - as I was. The difference was that I knew it now. I drove home quite subdued, ran a bath and sank into the warm water, feeling cleansed, warm and safe.

Over the next few weeks, my outlook on life changed completely. My food tastes changed overnight too. I'd been struggling to lose weight for many years, but now it was happening. I hadn't had a drink for many years because I seemed to have become sensitive to it, feeling ill whenever I drank. But now I bought a bottle of wine and started drinking a tiny amount every night. I started to live a little. I had always found social gatherings difficult because I felt inadequate, not knowing what to say. I wasn't sure who would want to speak to me since my life contains only spooky stuff and not many people want to discuss that. So I'd stayed away from social functions or kept quiet. Now I wanted to go out and talk to people. It was as if I had woken from a long slumber, yawned, peered over the wall and said, "Right, what have I missed?" For a while there was very little spirit work going on for me. It was like they knew that I needed to re-group, so I did just that.

I realised that I couldn't be there for everyone and just needed a little rest, so I took it. I had some days off work and started to write this book. The words flowed more easily than I ever thought possible. I started to understand what my life was about! The more I paid attention to myself and lived and had fun, the easier my life became and balance manifested more and more. I realised that I don't have to rush around chasing my tail every day; I can choose to go slower, it's ok to do that… what a revelation! We choose the life we have and we can just as easily choose not to have it. Anything is possible. You just have to hold that thought and believe it, then take the necessary steps. It's not that 'we cannot', it's that 'we will not' - that's the problem. But I'm so glad that 'they' tried to convince me, and that I fought and cried and suffered such loss and unhappiness, because it makes me who I am.

The story of my Mum now seems to have come full circle. Through all her hardship, she is still as feisty as ever. It took until she was seventy-six years old for her to hear the spirit world. One day we'd been talking about my spiritual experiences as a child, about how I'd heard and seen so much and yet she'd had no evidence at all. I didn't know why. I told her it was just the way it was. That evening, she decided to stay over at my house and we slept in the same room. Here is her account of what happened.

"About 2.30 a.m. I was woken by a loud bang from downstairs, like a back door banging against a wall. Then I remembered that Jacqui doesn't have a back door. I lay there very quietly, listening. I raised my head and looked at Jacqui. She hadn't stirred at all. I was now wondering if I was imagining it, so I closed my eyes and relaxed. Within seconds I heard someone on the stairs, climbing them very slowly. I turned to look at the door. No light was on in the house and no light shone under the door. Whoever it was, they reached the top of the stairs and stamped along the landing, turned the light on and off and went into the bathroom.

"I knew there was only myself, Jacqui and Rob in the house and that Rob was sleeping peacefully elsewhere. So who was it? I started to get quite uncomfortable at this point - I felt very nervous and considered waking Jacqui. If this was spirit then why was I hearing it and not her? I sat on the edge of the bed in the dark, just listening. All became silent so I got back into bed and tried to relax, moved onto my other side and looked at Jacqui. She has a red night light by her bed that was shining a small glow around her.

"Near to the bed is an en-suite. This door was opening slowly, on its own. I watched it, my heart in my mouth, not quite believing what I was seeing. I was petrified, I couldn't move. It was like I was meant to see this. When the door was fully open, it slammed with a force that shook the whole room. I jumped out of bed and shook Jacqui awake. I have never been so frightened in my life. If I'd ever been in any doubt that something else existed, I no longer doubted now. One thing I knew for sure - I would not be staying there again! To this day I still can't believe I actually experienced this."

When Mum woke me she was nearly hysterical. I couldn't understand what she was saying - door, stairs, bang? When I managed to calm her, she explained and I did feel for her. I had to go out onto the landing and explain to her that there was "Nothing there now", just as she did to me when I was a child. She now knew how I felt and understood that I'd told her the truth. It was a sobering moment for both of us. I don't know why it happened then, though we had discussed these things earlier in the day. Maybe they were listening? I have to admit it made me smile, and I wanted to punch the air with joy – vindicated at last! Welcome to my life.

We never know when proof will come to us, so we must walk forward every day knowing that spirit surrounds us. Change is possible in all our lives. We just need to accept that the spirit world can be here and now, and see what effect it has for each one of us. We are all dancers to our own tunes and actors in our own plays. Let's make this our best performance.

May your angels always keep you safe.

We are part of everything we have ever loved and I think it's those loves that form the tissue, if you like, of our acts of belief and faith. Acting is all about faith. Performing is an act of faith… That's why when the atheist says, "What if life's pointless? What if it's all a joke?" it has to be answered by the comedian, "Well if it's a joke, let's make it a good one!"

—KENNETH WILLIAMS

Lightning Source UK Ltd.
Milton Keynes UK
UKOW031610120513

210551UK00004B/40/P